All of Us Together

All of Us Together

The Story of Inclusion at the Kinzie School

Jeri Banks

Gallaudet University Press • Washington, D.C.

Gallaudet University Press, Washington, D.C. 20002

© 1994 by Gallaudet University. All rights reserved
Published 1994
Printed in the United States of America

Library of Congress Cataloging-in-Publication Data

Banks, Jeri.
    All of us together : the store of inclusion at the Kinzie School /
Jeri Banks.
        p.   cm.
    ISBN 1-56368-028-9 (alk. paper) : $24.95
        1. Kinzie School (Chicago, Ill.)   2. Deaf—Education—Illinois—Chicago—Case
studies.   3. Mainstreaming in education—Illinois—Chicago—Case studies.
HV2561.I483C43   1994
371.91′2′0977311—dc20   94-7508
                                                                        CIP

For
Liesl, Kristen, Rachel,
Max and the Kinzie Community,
with special appreciation to
the Golden Apple Foundation

The Kinzie kaleidoscope,
separate sparkles of color,
individual hues,
touching,
intermingling
into an intricate design,
constant for a point in time
but sensitive,
responsive to movement,
dynamically
dividing,
and reconnecting,
contouring new configurations
which slip easily
into another overall pleasing pattern
for a point in time,
everchanging
but always surrounded
by the supportive framework.

John H. Kinzie School is a public elementary school located on the southwest side of Chicago. Its total enrollment of 450 students includes a special education population of 135 children. Some of these youngsters have severe learning disabilities and communication disorders, but the majority have either severe or profound sensorineural hearing losses.

The Chicago school system categorizes those students with severe to profound losses, who cannot use their hearing to learn but must use vision instead, as *deaf*. Children with mild or moderate losses, whose hearing is functional with or without a hearing aid, are called *hard of hearing*. Chicago provides separate educational programs for deaf children and for hard of hearing students.

Kinzie Elementary School has a regular educational program that includes children from pre-kindergarten through eighth grade. Kinzie's deaf students enroll in its nursery at age three and continue until age fourteen, when they go on to high school.

The characters in Kinzie's story are named as they are called by the children. "Ms.," "Mrs.," and "Mr." are very difficult for young deaf children to articulate so teachers most frequently choose to use just their last names (Brownell, Banks). If the last name is difficult (Wysinski, Strablenka), the first name is used (Flo, Glor). The names of most of the characters in this narrative have been changed.

This is the story of one school that accepted students with disabilities. In the decade from 1982 to 1992, Kinzie School moved from two separate departments, regular education and special education, to a community of unconditional mainstreaming, that is, a school where every child feels he or she belongs. Creating this environment required working within the system, around it, and even against it. It is the story of ordinary people, a principal, teachers, parents, and students who believe that different kinds of people can live and work together and accomplish good things.

[M]ainstreaming means the valuing of human differences. It means that everyone is a teacher and that everyone is a learner. It means that all of us together are greater than any one of us or some of us.

Keith E. Beery, "Mainstreaming: A Problem and an Opportunity for General Education," *Focus on Exceptional Children* 6(1974): 6.

All of Us Together

CHAPTER 1

They invaded our school, each deaf boy and girl with a walkman on his chest and headphones over his ears. They wiggled their fingers, made strange noises, were always touching each other. But they stayed at their end of the building. They didn't go outside for recess. They walked with their teachers to and from the buses. They didn't have lunch with us either. They ate with their teachers too.

Their side of the building was a mystery. There were lots of pictures in their rooms, on the walls, on the blackboards, hanging on chart stands. And they had carpeting on the floors and drapes and new shades on the windows. Their rooms looked happy.

Their teachers were kind of loud and dramatic; they exaggerated what they said. We could hear them beating drums and ringing bells. They were noisy and they laughed a lot.

                                        Rachel, eighth grade

Two separate worlds, regular and special education. The regular education teachers were veterans. They had done it all, produced winning math, science, and writing projects, created beautiful art displays. They had had the students who could do it all. Of 497 Chicago public schools, John H. Kinzie was one of the twenty in which children achieved average reading gains of more than one year. This was the edge of the city, out past Midway Airport, the far southwestern boundary, the country club.

Their principal, affectionately called "the Polish Pope," pontificated over his three hundred novices at the front door each morning. He had seen his teachers do it all. He took pride in their accomplishments and in the fact that not a single bureaucratic form ever lingered on his desk.

But the graffiti was on the brickwork. He was witness to the changes in the high school next door. In 1975 he had ordered his teachers to lock their doors against riotous adolescents running wildly through the halls of that adjacent building. He heard recurring reports of assault, battery, and disorderly conduct. Black and white high school students were clashing on their common grounds. The horrible monster of urban problems, spawned in the troubled backwaters of the inner city, was extending its tentacles even to his playground.

Once packed to capacity, his own school dwindled in enrollment to just one room of each grade. The brightest students, with the most upwardly mobile parents, transferred each September to suburban schools farther southwest in Burbank, Bridgeview, or Oak Lawn. Others, unable to move away, congregated instead in the peaceful parochial schools nearby.

The neighborhood housed mainly wary senior citizens who tended their gardens and swept the alleys behind their brick bungalows. They were holding onto one of Chicago's few traditional "neighborhoods." Their lives centered on their churches and on Archer Avenue, where, between the savings and loans, in the mom-and-pop stores and the ethnic restaurants, they could still buy *pierogis* and *kolackis*. The older residents hadn't been here when Archer Avenue was an Indian trail, but some could remember the quiet farmlands and swamps. Their families had arrived when the biggest industry was truck farming, and produce was driven into the Halsted Street markets.

An Interview with a Kinzie Neighbor

When Gertrude was a little girl, there were street cars and no cars. In her yard she had goats and chickens. Most houses were made out of wood, and there were no sidewalks. There was outside plumbing, no television or water heaters. She had no basement or den. They bought vegetables and ice from people who came to everybody's door. They carried milk in wagons. They had radios that you listened to only with ear phones.

Gertrude was born in 1906. She had three brothers and two sisters. Her father's name was Robert. He worked for the B & O Railroad. Her mother's name was Gertrude. She was a housewife.

Gertrude has been living in the same house for sixty-four years. Now she is the oldest person on the block. Back then there was only one house on each block. The president's name was Theodore Roosevelt. The city was just about all farm land.

Dominic, third grade

Their area was called "Clearing" after the huge railroad freight clearing yard opened just before the turn of the century. In 1926 airplanes swooped over the trains, and more of the farmland was replaced by the concrete runways of Midway Airport. After World War II, the fields totally disappeared. Two-flat and four-flat apartment buildings and single-family, cozy Georgian homes rose up to house neighboring Garfield Ridge residents, more than tripling the area population. Bustling Midway soon became the busiest airport in the world, and families traveled from all parts of the city to spend Saturday evenings or Sunday afternoons watching the planes take off and land. These families also came to Archer Avenue to shop for Communion and bridal dresses, or to spend their savings on end tables and love seats.

But the prosperity generated by the airport was short-lived. In the 1960s O'Hare International Airport appropriated Midway's traffic and later, its title. Business slumped; shops of all kinds abandoned once-thriving Cicero Avenue. The sounds of the seventies diminished to a few Midway flights a day buzzing the sturdy bungalows.

Some of the aging homeowners welcomed back their divorced children and their grandchildren. Chicago policemen, firemen, and other municipal workers, required to live in the city, still bought houses here. And the community's ethnic tradition offered a welcome mat to new immigrants from Poland. But altogether their children filled only half of the Kinzie Elementary School building.

Permissive transfers, waivers that offered some minority children an alternative to their highly segregated neighborhood schools, began to arrive from the Chicago Board of Education's Department of Equal Educational Opportunity Programs. The school system's response to the 1980 Justice Department consent decree mandating desegregation, these forms piled up on the principal's desk. African American and Latino children came on the bus to participate in the Options Program, a specialty offering in academics, the arts, or computer technology. At Kinzie the incentive was instrumental music, a chance to play in a band.

The board's goal was "to establish the greatest practicable number of stably desegregated schools despite Chicago's extreme housing segregation." Kinzie, with its 80-percent-white student population, was targeted to increase its minority enrollment to at least 30 percent in order to become "a stably desegregated school." A few black teachers were forcibly transferred in, a few white teachers forcibly transferred out. Students and staff played musical chairs to the ballad of the Desegregation Plan. It was the board's exercise in composition, an attempt to create harmony among its citywide 61 percent African American, 17 percent white, and 20 percent Latino student population. Kinzie's principal, finding his desk becoming a clutter of unsettling forms, opted for the clear expanses of the golf greens.

A younger man came, bred of "good old boy," Irish-principal stock, a kind of Gentleman Jim Corbett with his mustache and monogrammed cuffs. Tall, trim, in appearance the paragon of professionalism, James Franklin dressed like a corporate CEO, always the matching silk handkerchief folded in his breast pocket. A new principal, eager to assume command, he found himself the captain of a ship with the admiral on board. He had to share his building with Ms. Alice T. Altschuler, the dour district superintendent whose office had been poured with the foundation. She had been principal of Kinzie School just a quarter of a century earlier, and then she had been administrator of the adjoining high school. Now, as superintendent, both schools were her domain.

Ms. Altschuler, as a no-nonsense college advisor, had supervised the student teaching practicums of half the teachers in the city. Her reputation was integrally and indelibly woven into the school system's folklore. Although certainly past retirement age, she appeared a healthy middle-aged matron. Her square face, a picture of pinched superiority, was framed by a suitable blend of red-brown and gray hair, in a conservative, beauty shop molding. A scarf, in quiet colors, always accented her three-piece outfits. Ms. Altschuler's exact age was one of the most sought after secrets in District 18. But in her administrative oxfords, she moved swiftly and silently through Kinzie's halls, like a shark, sporadically accosting some poor fish who had the incredibly bad timing to cross her territory with a coffee cup in hand. She could still strike terror in students and teachers alike during any fire drill that didn't measure up to her standards.

September, 1982

Dear Parents and Friends of Kinzie School:

Our school welcomes the addition this year of 15 divisions of deaf youngsters who have been transferred here. The cooperative efforts of the new staff with the previously existing staff have resulted in the minimizing of disruption to either program. We feel that the positive manner in which this major program change is being accomplished highlights the adaptability of the school in this, its 25th anniversary year.

James P. Franklin

The new principal filled the vacant classrooms with special education students, a whole deaf department. The community was pleased that these children would occupy the empty rooms. The outsiders would be learning in separate classes on their own side of the building. Neighborhood residents were sympathetic to these transferring students of all colors because they were handicapped. Their teachers were saints.

It was hard for the parents to understand, however, the renovation that took place in half of the school building. Although it was discussed at a Parents Club meeting, most didn't understand why the newcomers got carpeting, drapes, and new shades. They were told that the deaf children needed a quiet environment for learning. It didn't make sense to them. If the children were deaf, they couldn't hear and they couldn't talk. It was hard for the neighbors to accept this extravagant redecorating in the special education classrooms when their own children's rooms had torn shades, chipped floor tiles, and walls grimy with the accumulated dirt of twenty years. Some of the children's feelings reflected their parents' disapproval.

> When the deaf children first came to our school, I felt jealousy, resentment, and threatened that they would affect our school life and take over our school. I was prejudiced toward the deaf. I felt, "Who cares, I'm not deaf!"
>
> Tara, seventh grade

Ms. Altschuler approved the move. Decreasing enrollment had created the real possibility that Kinzie School would be closed and her district offices uprooted. The arrival of the deaf divisions resolved her major concern. In addition, the deaf population, being a quiet group, would create no administrative problems, no disciplinary disturbances, no staff complaints, and no parental involvement. Although Ms. Altschuler's official statements were supportive of special education, her unofficial comments conveyed her belief that serious education occurred only in the regular classrooms. Special education watered down the process, advocated learning by doing, even playing games. To her the rationale for reduced class size was tenuous.

The veterans also knew that serious education occurred only in the regular classrooms. There was no comparing the amount of energy expended teaching a group of eight handicapped children with the work involved in managing a regu-lar class of thirty. And how the regular classes had changed in the span of their careers! Gone were the children eager to list the natural resources of the Mississippi Valley or to create a shoe box diorama of ancient Rome. Now their students looked to school for security, a place to get breakfast, lunch, and a respite from their home lives, which sometimes rivaled television shows in their violence. These pupils looked to teachers for support, not stimulation. They were already chal-lenged too much by alcoholic fathers, emotionally stressed mothers, truant older brothers, demanding younger sisters who were their responsibilities from three until seven each evening. For some, the problems in their math books were as far removed as this school was from the problems in their neighborhoods, where gangs and drug dealers were lurking. The teachers knew there were no regular classes anymore. They taught thirty or more students handicapped by the soci-ety in which they lived. Some teachers quietly but bitterly offered an open invitation to the special education teachers to work with their regular classes, to experience how challeng-ing teaching really could be.

Others coveted the special education resource room full of colorful programs and stimulating teaching kits purchased with federal funds. Accustomed to spending their own money on duplicating books, bulletin board displays, and supplies, and used to sharing equipment that might or might not be in working order, veteran teachers saw that the special educa-tion teachers had phonographs, filmstrip machines, and over-head projectors. They had numerous duplicating workbooks and a solid collection of filmstrips and storybooks. The deaf students didn't use the standard textbooks.

But the resources of the deaf department were untouch-able, purchased with funds distributed exclusively for students with disabilities. Its instructional decisions were made by special education personnel. A released assistant principal and team leader came with the deaf department. They received orders from the coordinator of the Deaf and Hard-of-Hearing Program for the south side of the city, the coordinator for the Physically Handicapped, and the Special Education director, whose directives were certified, in turn, by the assistant superintendent of Pupil Personnel Services and Special Education, the deputy superintendent of Field Management, and the deputy superintendent of Education Services.

The special education coordinators made board procedure clear to Mr. Franklin immediately. Even though the deaf children sat at desks in his building, he needn't be concerned about their management. The coordinators pointed out that educating deaf students was not his field of expertise. His role was to provide spelling paper, pencils, art materials, chalk, toilet tissue, and furniture. And he was expected to solve the interminable bus problems. In matters of curriculum, the deaf department would run itself. Two principals in previous schools understood this policy. The deaf department had always run itself.

CHAPTER 2

I went to the Arts Festival. I am a ballerina, and I danced on the stage with other girls. I saw a mime, and she was very nice. I talked to her. I also saw crafts and paintings. I would like to go to the Arts Festival again.

Trina, deaf

I was a teacher of the deaf, the group speech-and-auditory-training teacher. The children called me Banks and simultaneously signed a *B* in a circular motion in front of the mouth. (*Mrs.,* with its double syllables of sibilant *s,* was an impossibility for the younger children.) Every class in the deaf department came to me for forty minutes a week of group instruction in speaking and listening skills: speech, speech-reading, and auditory training. This period, along with two gym classes, provided the three mandated preparation times for classroom teachers.

I was not a speech therapist. I had taken the one speech class in the teacher training sequence required for certification. I used the Chicago Board of Education's Speech Curriculum for the Hearing Impaired as my guide. At the same time I dovetailed each child's Individual Educational Plan (IEP), with its personalized speech goals and short-term objectives, into the continuum of the curriculum. Folders of checklists for my one-hundred-plus students tumbled over in heaps beside my "speech" chair, my find. It had wheels, and that made it easy for me to roll right up to within inches of one of the eight boys and girls seated in a semicircle facing me. To achieve an *f* sound, I might have to lift a child's fingers in front of my own lips so that he would feel the steady stream of air or experience the contrasting explosion for a *p.*

Teaching speech was best done close up, one-on-one or maybe -two. Authorities on teaching speech to deaf children, such as Daniel Ling, recommended short periods of instruction interspersed and reinforced throughout the day, a quick drill before the children lined up for lunch, again while they were waiting for the bathroom. The standard forty-minute period was the least desirable arrangement, but there was the problem of organization. Classroom teachers needed periods without any children in front of them; time to prepare, time to review IEPs.

Always searching for a better way, my colleagues and I had bought Ling's book and were meeting one morning each week before school started, to come to an understanding of his methods and to determine how best we could apply them to our own program. It was common knowledge that teachers of deaf students felt more inadequate about teaching speech than about any other subject. Yet, up until just a decade earlier, the Chicago system had advocated a strictly oral approach to communication. Sign language was added during the 1970s; it didn't replace speech but was used in combination with it, "total communication." Teachers still had a strong motivation to help their children attain intelligible speech and to be able to speechread English. But their efforts were none too successful. Recent studies, like past ones, revealed that only one word in five spoken by deaf children could be understood by listeners unfamiliar with their speech. And the children in these studies had been learning how to speak from infancy throughout their elementary grades.

Motivation wasn't enough; it took drill, drill, drill. I conceded some of my class period to the droning "ba(r), baw, boo, bee, fa(r), faw, foo, fee, pa(r), paw, poo, pee" of phonetic speech drills (Practice not until it's right, but until it's never wrong), but I sandwiched in poems and songs.

> One, two,
> One, two
> I love you.
> Yes, I do.

The seasons changed but the melody remained the same. Sung to the tune of "Frere Jacques":

> It is Autumn!
> It is Autumn!
> Summer's gone,
> Summer's gone,
> Wintertime is coming.
> Wintertime is coming.
> It won't be long.

> It is winter!
> It is winter!
> Autumn's gone,
> Autumn's gone,
> Springtime will be coming.
> Springtime will be . . .

I liked to try new things, to stage little performances. Playing the triangles in a primary assembly was one of my own earliest school memories. One Christmas at the Marquette School, the deaf students in my speech classes presented "The Nutcracker Suite." It was classic elementary school theatrics, crepe paper waltzing flowers and hyperactive garbage bag mice. But it was the Sugar Plum Fairy who stole the show. All I heard in the halls afterward was "I want to dance too!"

I started meeting with five deaf girls, ten-year-olds, for a ballet class. We all gave up our lunch once a week, pushed the chairs and desks aside in my classroom; the oak floors were splendid. I hadn't danced since college, eighteen years ago, and with the birth of each of my four children had come some extra weight. Backstage at the ballet, I'd probably be taken for the costume lady rather than the ballet mistress; nevertheless, with a little energy and effort, I could open the curtains to the world of dance. There was nothing to lose but pounds.

The girls were enthusiastic but uncoordinated. We began with the basics: arm and foot positions, stretching, and moving in fundamental ways, no fancy French terms. We danced to music, classical and popular. The girls could hear some of the musical frequencies and feel the rhythmic vibrations from the boom box on the floor.

Angela, a chunky black girl, could hear almost none of the music and moved in a downright clumsy fashion, but she always had a beaming smile on her face. She seemed to be enjoying herself so much that you had to applaud her performance. Maria, by contrast, benefited enormously from using her hearing aid; shy but lithe, she moved easily to the music. Doreen, tall, leggy, black, and beautiful, had very little hearing but moved with a natural grace. Rosalie, so thin that she looked brittle, seemed to gain some strength through her movements, a complete contrast to Ana, who had a sparkle in her dark, Spanish eyes and the energy of a gymnast. Each girl approached dance in a unique way determined as much by her motivation and prowess as by the amount of residual hearing she had. At the end of the semester, although they were timid, the dancers demonstrated their skills for their classmates, performed a simple combination, and convinced the administrators that their class had some merit.

The next year we were allotted the last thirty minutes of

the week, and every girl in the deaf department was an aspiring ballerina. Ballet became a reward for making satisfactory academic progress and behaving acceptably.

But the girls progressed in dance too. They gained in confidence and agility and in the spring danced at the Arts in Education Week festivities downtown. They wore leotards and circle skirts sewn by teachers and parents. Their sign and dance performance of "You Light Up My Life" earned them a standing ovation from the warm and accepting lunchtime audience of relatives, office workers, and retirees. Their photograph appeared in the *Sun Times*; they were celebrities!

The dance program continued in the new school. The Kinzie Deaf Dance Class expanded to the last forty-minute period on Friday and to all the deaf girls in the department aged six through eleven. We met in the multipurpose room, a kind of cafetorium where folding lunch tables lined the walls and there was a tiny stage. In a good week thirty girls might be allowed to participate.

During the holidays Mr. Franklin invited the dance class to entertain the Parents Club. Kinzie's PC was a small, close-knit group of very involved parents who ran three major events: the annual candy sale, the school picnic, and the graduation party. They were exclusively mothers of hearing students, and most had two or three children in the school. A few had even graduated from Kinzie themselves. Ms. Masters, their leader, kept informed about educational topics, was active in other community organizations, and had a keen political sense as well.

They all enjoyed the dance performance and during the punch and cookies expressed an interest in having their own girls participate in the class. Everyone agreed that it was a good idea to include hearing girls in the deaf dance class.

And so some regular and special education students came together for the first time.

When I grow up I want to dance
So I could visit other countries like France.
I would get a standing ovation
For my own dance creation.
The President would shake my hand
And say my performance was grand.
I would dance on a huge stage,
And the audience would be amazed.
I would eat healthy food and get plenty of rest
So when I'm on stage, I'll do my very best.

Dina, fifth grade

The Kinzie Integrated Dance Class welcomed fourth-grade girls the first year. The deaf girls had the advantage; they were already dancers, and some could speechread well. The hearing girls were tentative; dancing was new, and they didn't know sign language. I was comfortable with the class; before becoming certified to teach deaf classes, I had substituted as a "day-to-day" in many of the schools on the southwest side, in all of the grades. And there was no choice in dance class; you had to keep moving. The girls liked the popular music of their dance, "Heart Light," so they put up with the choreography, which required that they be partners, a deaf and hearing girl in each pair.

When the invitation arrived to perform at the opening ceremonies of Arts in Education Week in 1983, the girls found they had something in common—nervousness. They had to work together so that they all looked good. Parents and teachers sewed more circle skirts, and Ms. Masters arranged for hamburgers, fries, and a bus after school. Local celebrities and artists crowded the impressive main hall of Chicago's Cultural Center. As the girls climbed into the spotlight on the tiny platform, stage fright and bravado tumbled in the blenders of their emotions. But they captured the hearts of their audience when, in the middle of the dance, they flipped over the red-and-yellow felt "heart lights" pinned to the inside of their leotards. Warm feelings flooded the gathering, making the Kinzie dancers, parents, teachers, and principal proud. Ms. Altschuler wasn't there, but Dr. Ruth Love, the general superintendent, congratulated the girls and posed for a photo with their group. Mr. Franklin had taken a risk in sending his students downtown after school, but every child had a guardian in attendance to take her home that night, an accomplishment in itself.

What do dancers get when they eat too much? Ballet aches (belly aches)
Where do fortune tellers dance? At the crystal ball.
Jennifer, deaf

CHAPTER 3

Gray is
. . . the sidewalk leading to education,
all cracked and patchy.

Nicky, seventh grade

The deaf children needed expensive equipment in addition to the carpeting and drapery that helped to muffle the environmental noises in the classroom—the feet scuffling across the floor, chairs dragging, desks banging, books dropping, kids talking. Although they were identified as deaf, the children had varying degrees of hearing loss classified from moderate to profound. (Chicago's children with mild hearing losses were enrolled in hard-of-hearing classes provided in schools separate from the deaf.) All had sensorineural hearing losses, damage to their inner ears, nerve injury that could not be repaired. But almost all had some degree of residual hearing.

As their first priority the special education teachers attempted to maximize the use of that residual hearing for learning language. Students deaf from birth had never heard themselves babbling and their parents jibberjabbering back over their cribs. They had never received those basic messages like "time to eat," "look at the doggie," and "I love you." When they got hearing aids, sometimes as an infant, but most often not until age two or three, the jibberjabbering finally began.

More than 90 percent of Kinzie's deaf students had parents who were not deaf. These parents told heartbreaking stories of making the rounds of clinics and doctors' offices before they received a definitive diagnosis of hearing loss. Sometimes they were told to wait and see, and they waited too long and saw more than they could understand. They were devastated by the revelation of the handicap and frustrated by their inability to communicate with their children. Unlike the children of deaf parents, who were nurtured in sign language from the day they were born, children of hearing parents often went without any formal language system until they arrived in school at age three. More fortunate were the few children who were identified early and attended parent-infant clinics.

Once these children were in school, their teachers attempted to inundate them with signs and spoken language appropriately amplified. A systematic program of speech instruction and auditory training began immediately. A group FM network allowed each classroom teacher to transmit messages from his or her own microphone by means of a class frequency directly to each student's receiver unit. This eliminated the problems of background noise, reverberation, and poor signal-to-noise ratio. (When children were wearing their own personal aids, they could hear the teacher's voice less clearly as he or she moved further away from them and their aids' microphones.)

The FM systems had a few bugs. Albert spent most of one morning listening to a teacher in another classroom, and several students were bombarded by weird video game noises. The beeping sounds caused by interference from nearby hospital pagers were quickly eliminated by changing the class frequency. No one ever got the anticipated transmission, "Midway 371, clear to land, 22 right."

The board of education purchased auditory training units

but neglected to allocate money for their maintenance or repair. Real teaching was impeded by the inevitable breakdown in equipment. Despite numerous requests to the special education bureaucracy over a period of five months, no funds were released and none were projected to be forthcoming. I complained to Mr. Franklin about the utter futility of teaching speech and listening skills without amplification. He suggested that I explain the problem to the Parents Club, that I demonstrate a speech and auditory training lesson at their next meeting. Then Mr. Franklin distributed a school newsletter.

April, 1983

Dear Parents and Friends of Kinzie School:

Kinzie School has been enriched by the addition, this school year, of fifteen divisions of deaf children to our student body. The nature of these students' disability dictates that they have certain special equipment in order that we may fulfill our commitment to provide them with an appropriate education. One such piece of equipment is called a phonic ear auditory training unit. A number of those units were removed from the school for repair in December. Those units are not yet returned because the Board of Education has not provided money for the necessary repairs.

Our efforts to have these units repaired and returned to Kinzie have so far proved fruitless. We know that all of our parents believe in a quality education for every Kinzie student; therefore, we are asking each parent to write a letter to the General Superintendent asking

for the release of money to repair the Auditory Training Units. Letters should be addressed to
Dr. Ruth B. Love
General Superintendent of Schools
218 N. LaSalle St., Chicago, IL 60601

Dr. Love's office referred the parents' letters to Frances Wood, the coordinator of Physically Handicapped Programs. From her, the letters went to Jane Blatt, the coordinator of Hearing-Impaired Programs on the south side of the city. Ms. Blatt then called Ms. Altschuler and informed her that one of District 18's principals was stirring up parents.

Miss Altschuler was enraged; one of *her* principals had violated the chain of command, the modus operandi. If teachers had problems, they were to bring them to their principals. Principals addressed their district superintendents, who approached the associate superintendent, who had access to the general superintendent. Of course, there were also the intermediaries to be consulted, coordinators, directors, and assistant superintendents in numerous specialties.

Ms. Altschuler's response was not to address the need for hearing aid equipment but to focus on Mr. Franklin's lack of understanding of "how things are done." In a conference in his office, she delivered a lengthy monologue punctuated by pauses in which Mr. Franklin was expected to nod appropriately. Like a naughty boy, his eyes assented, "Yes, I hear you." But behind his eyes he registered, "Never, yes, I agree with you."

Ms. Altschuler's soft but steely voice at times appeared to ramble, yet there was a subtle measure to the stress of certain words. In spite of her obfuscation, the message coalesced. "Never make waves, never cause a superior to have to make a difficult decision." There was the golden rule. A good principal considered his or her actions not in terms of what is best for the children, but in light of what is expedient for administrators.

Ms. Blatt also telephoned Mr. Franklin. Neither did she address the need for hearing aid equipment but instead complained about the deluge of letters that her secretary was now forced to answer. She observed that in an incredibly ungrateful manner, one of her own teachers of the deaf had instigated this disruption in her office by explaining to the parents the dilemma of teaching children speech and auditory discrimination without amplification.

And had everyone forgotten that it was Ms. Blatt who had initiated moving staff and students from the chaos of their overcrowded rooms to these pleasant surroundings at Kinzie? She had scrutinized the labyrinthine lines of items in the monstrous board of education budget and found the allowance to allocate monies for carpeting, drapery, and equipment. She had created a model environment for teaching deaf children on the south side of Chicago. Some of the city's other deaf centers still had doubled up classes; even the well-known Alexander Graham Bell School on the north side had classes sharing rooms. All were still using the antiquated larger hearing aid units that were breaking down rapidly. There was no money to be found for replacing these old aids, let alone for repairing Kinzie's new models. It was selfish of the Kinzie staff to demand even more funds, but because they had called attention to themselves, the money for repairs had to be found. The parents' letters had finally settled on Ms. Blatt's desk, in a neat bundle, topped with a directive from Dr. Love to expedite. Representatives from the Parents Club had not only written, but Ms. Masters had also led a group downtown to address the board of education meeting. They had demonstrated not for their own children, but for *the invaders in the carpeted rooms.*

Dear Parents and Friends of Kinzie School:

In last month's newsletter, we asked parents to write to Dr. Love requesting the provision of funds to repair auditory equipment for our deaf students. Those letters had the hoped-for effect; the repaired units will very shortly be returned to our school. In as much as Dr. Love responded so positively and promptly to our request, it would now be appropriate for us to express our appreciation to her.

James P. Franklin

CHAPTER 4

I know a boy who can not hear,
He wears a button in his ear.

Kari, third grade

Every deaf child had a personal hearing aid—on paper there was a serial number or two for each. Most children had body aids that were worn on the chest in a harness: standard white cotton, cool blue denim, or far-out crocheted. Usually about eight square inches in size, the rectangular hearing aid unit housed a battery-powered transmitter with a microphone on top, situated in the direct path of falling cookie crumbs and spaghetti noodles. Two cords, often badly chewed, connected the transmitter to receiver buttons in the ears. The receivers snapped onto custom-fitting earmolds that fit into the ear canal forming a tight seal and eliminating any annoying squealing feedback sounds. Some students, mostly older, had one or two ear-level aids that, worn behind the ear, were much less conspicuous and more likely to slip off and be flushed down the toilet. The microphone and transmitter rested in a small plastic casing only about an inch and a half in length.

It has been documented that on any given school day less than 25 percent of children's hearing aids are in good working order. That's even with the "smiley button system": Kinzie's teachers greeted their charges each day with "Good Morning," followed by, "Did you wear your hearing aid?" A hearing aid in the school bag got a sad face and an emphatic shaking index finger, "Naughty, naughty! You wear your hearing aid! It's important! Tell Mommy, '*Put on my hearing aid!*' "

No hearing aid called for melodrama. "Where's your hearing aid? *You forgot! You don't know! In the drawer! You need your hearing aid! It's important!* That's awful! Tell Mommy, 'I need my hearing aid.' " A child signing "store" evoked despair if he had worn his aid on a recent school day or resignation if the aid was habitually missing. "In the shop? When will Mommy get it? Tomorrow? You said that two weeks ago."

With a visible hearing aid, the student faced a warm smile, maybe even a hug. "Is your hearing aid working? Can you hear me?" The answer "yes" merited one smiley face on the chart. Five smiley faces in a week won the smiley button for the day and a pretzel. No smiley face for missing battery, battery in backwards, or dead battery. Damage deeper than a cord meant distress: a series of phone calls and notes to mother, grandmother, the baby-sitter, the preschool, the school nurse and social worker (both only part-time staff), the audiologist (on hand once a week but usually too busy testing), the child's clinic, hearing aid dealer, Division of Services for Crippled Children (DSCC), and maybe even Division of Children and Family Services (DCFS).

Kinzie students now had their school auditory-training units back in good repair, but the board of education never arranged for earmolds to be fitted to these aids. There were no funds. Children used the earmolds from their personal aids when they had them. If they didn't, the school had a very limited number of medium-weight, sweaty, squealy earphones. Growing youngsters needed new earmolds frequently, sometimes after only six months; as their ears grew, the molds became loose and the annoying whistling began to interfere with their reception. "I hear a hearing aid. Whose hearing aid is that?" became an integral part of the daily lesson.

Kinzie was uniquely lucky to have Siegel Institute of Michael Reese Hospital agree to make earmold impressions right on the school premises. The logistics were organized by Siegel audiologist Theresa Jabaly and myself. In a wonderful adoptive gesture, Dr. Jeantet, an otolaryngologist compassionate enough to do fifty ear, nose, and throat examinations for a cup of tea and some toast, and the audiologists who came gratis actually set up an ENT clinic in a classroom. School and medical personnel gathered data and completed forms for reimbursement for the earmolds using green card—public aid card—numbers. Parents who could afford it paid, but 90 percent of Kinzie's deaf students were on public aid. Their hearing aids, which cost about $350, were purchased with the assistance of the Division of Services for Crippled Children. A pair of earmolds on this special day could be ordered for $20, half the standard price.

The familiar environment of school diminished but didn't eliminate all of the bawling and squirming that occurred as the liquid and powder concoction was mixed and poured into the children's ears to form the impressions. Understanding that it was painless but frightening for some youngsters, like visiting the dentist, teachers made a special effort to explain the process and offer support, especially to the youngest ones. Most of the older kids had experienced many times having new earmolds made and were pleased to get out of math or written language for half an hour. In some cases models of bravery were chosen to accompany the timorous, but on a few occasions the selections backfired. There was one chain reaction of tantrums that surprised everyone when Brenton, a bully at age five and as tough as he was skinny, turned out to be a bigger baby than the three-year-olds in his company. An exhausting session with stubborn and very stocky four-year-old Kenith taught everyone the value of teamwork.

The earmold project proved to be a rare interagency event in which teacher, audiologist, and doctor were able to confer about the special needs of the child in their midst. Recommendations were made for hearing aid use, teachers were inserviced, and tips were traded on how to actually make contact with parents.

In the course of the day, as the teachers cradled their students over the basins and Dr. Jeantet washed the wax out of their ears, a small collection of oddities was removed. With the doctor's syringe came popcorn kernels and beads, the tiny objects that children tend to put in their ears or nose, and one cockroach. That critter, the constant and critical need for funding necessities such as earmolds, and an absurd release of tension led to a whimsical exercise in grant writing by the staff:

Teacher Incentive Program

Title: Determining the Frequency Range of Conductive Hearing Loss Due to Entomological Intrusions

Need: There is a gaping vacuum in the body of traditional research on conductive losses due to entomological intrusions in profoundly deaf, culturally disadvantaged, preschool and primary age children. Previous research seems to indicate that the *Blatta orientalis* (a common entomological intruder) may adversely affect low frequencies. According to earlier findings, *formicidae* seem to display a propensity for artificial hearing mechanisms. However, it has been hypothesized that cicada may destroy high frequency reception. As of this date, no definitive study has been done. This proposed research will fill the gaping vacuum.

Activities: Permission slips will be sent to the parents of the entire deaf population, including "deaf" teachers. Three days later, permission slips will be sent again. Seven days later, more permission slips will be sent and telephone calls made.

Audiologists will test the deaf population.

Otologists will examine the deaf population for entomological intruders.

Evaluation: School personnel will preserve samples and tabulate findings. Conclusions will be presented to professional periodicals and conventions for evaluation.

Costs: Skippy peanut butter jars for samples   free

      Examination lamp rental $19.95

      Otologists and audiologists   gratis

Staff Development at Condesa del Mar

    for participants $980.00

Total $999.95

Mr. Franklin is a good principal and he is funny. He has a good sense of humor.

Wayne, first grade

There were very few interruptions to the class-room schedule except for an intermittent "Mr. Franklin, call the office. Mr. Franklin, please call the office" from the public address system. Mr. Franklin was an exemplar of the management-by-walking-around theory of administration. After solving the morning's immediate problems—a student concealing a pocketknife, a bus driver suspected of drinking between runs, a grandparent complaining about too many prunes in the school lunches ("And we all know what prunes are good for!")—he began his rounds. At a leisurely pace he moved from room to room, beginning with the primary grades closest to the office, lingering in the pre-school classes and halls of the deaf wing, and finishing in the intermediate and upper grades on the second floor. In a non-threatening manner he greeted the teacher and often the class, shaking hands with the deaf children, calling the atten-tion of the hearing students to his tie or the surgical scars on his knee.

The ties, which seasonally sported pumpkins, reindeer, colored eggs, or flags, were most often gifts from the children. One fashion-conscious first grader, Darvonte, started a class counting-and-memory game: keeping a tally of just how many different patterned ties Mr. Franklin wore. While the primary children tabulated his neckties, the upper-grade stu-dents focused on his knee. During the week following his surgery, he managed to give every class a peek at his scars; and one science period was devoted to the video of his arthroscopy.

Mr. Franklin's slow gait, which some staff members called the "shillelagh shuffle," pounded a percussion that was easy to distinguish in the quiet halls. The beat of its approach meant one more minute for a teacher to straighten her back, widen her smile, or put an extra amount of enthusiasm into her presentation. After a short time, however, most of the staff became comfortable with his presence. Teachers invited him to view some "star" paper or listen to an exceptional recitation. Deaf children were eager to show him their Bulls, Bears, or Turtles shirts, new shoes, or current classroom project. Hearing children were anxious to tell him a story. They knew, however, if they missed this opportunity, they could approach him on the playground or in the lunchroom later. He was always available for at least a pat on the shoulder.

> This tall man has white and brown hair. He wears funny ties and hats that little kids make for him. He walks down the halls visiting classrooms, pretending that he knows all the answers to the questions that the teachers ask him. He quietly and quickly slips out of the room before the teachers can ask him something that he doesn't know. Then he goes to his office to talk to a little girl. He tells her, "So you're the one who gave me my white hair." Afterward he dismisses her and goes down the hall for another walk.
>
> Judy, eighth grade

Mr. Franklin was a listener. Staff member or student, adult down to preschooler, whoever had an honest concern could be assured of at least two minutes of his concentrated attention. Younger children could usually charm double the amount of time from him. And he followed through, too. If it was a task that should be done, and it could be done, he would see that it would be done.

For that purpose, Mr. Franklin always carried along a scratch pad with memos for specific teachers. He jotted down new concerns as he observed them. Making the rounds was his opportunity to monitor his program, to see if teachers were teaching, learners learning, and other staff members completing their assigned tasks, to see if classrooms looked inviting, if activities were engaging.

His cryptic observations clued teachers in to the serious side of his visits and elicited explanations, particularly about the hearing impaired classes. Special education teachers were eager to share background information and suggest readings—an article in the professional journals, *Volta Review,* or the *American Annals of the Deaf,* Joanne Greenberg's novel, *In This Sign.* If he was going to evaluate their performance, they wanted him to be as knowledgeable as possible.

And Mr. Franklin was eager to learn about deafness. In his five years of teaching he had encountered few special education students. As a district science coordinator, he came in contact with none. After passing the system's administration exam, Mr. Franklin bounced from one interim principal position to another, falling back into the classroom, and then rising to the main office again. For very brief periods he managed schools that serviced children with learning disabilities and behavior disorders. Kinzie School was Mr. Franklin's first permanent administrative assignment. Six months after his arrival, he accepted responsibility for a hundred children with hearing disabilities, a whole deaf department.

His teachers in the deaf department thought of themselves as "our side." They had all transferred to Kinzie together from a school in a changing neighborhood. When large numbers of Arabian families migrated to the Marquette Park area, the teachers' school building became so overcrowded that the deaf classes were forced to surrender half of their rooms. The departmental speech and art teachers had none; one traveled with a shopping bag, the other, a cart. Administrators, considering only numbers, combined two separate deaf classes into one classroom, a total of no more than twenty children. However, because these students varied widely in age and academic ability, it was impossible for teachers to team students for instruction. Moreover, the major focus of the educational programs of both teachers was teaching auditory discrimination and utilizing auditory cues for learning. Understanding one aural communication in a quiet environment is difficult enough for a deaf child, but with two classes working simultaneously, discriminating between two competing transmissions is impossible. How could any rational educator justify one classroom with two conflicting auditory signals being transmitted simultaneously? One teacher characterized the feelings of the majority when she said, "Moving to Kinzie was like dying and going to heaven."

"Our side" had experienced good times and bad times, deaths, births, illnesses, accidents, marriages and divorces, highs and lows with their children. Many of them had been teaching together for twenty years. The coffee pot in the team leader's room was their warm hearth, offering a spot to share a laugh, a worry, or an absurdity. Twice each day teachers had a ten minute break from the isolation of teaching, a break from the overwhelming task of trying to teach deaf children to speak a language they had never heard, to read without language. They struggled to beat the statistics indicating that the average deaf seventeen-year-old reads just beyond third-grade level compared to his hearing peer who reads beyond tenth, that the average hearing seven-year-old could guess and still obtain a score on a standardized reading test comparable to that of a deaf child who had been in school for fifteen years.

It was even more depressing knowing that for people who are deaf, reading is the most efficient and effective means of getting information. If only some researcher would give teachers the magic key to language. They had already tried a disappointing succession of communication doors within the short span of their careers. Speech along with speechreading was one avenue that, for most students, proved to be too obscure. Understanding a speaker's message by watching his mouth and face was an insurmountable task since only 30 percent of English sounds are visible on the lips.

Fingerspelling required too much fine-motor coordination for very young children and arthritic teachers. Signed English was broader and seemed to be the right entry until experts suggested that combining speech and signs created a processing overload for the brain. In addition, signing English at the rate of speaking it was impossible. Teachers either slowed down their instruction, or they transmitted information with omissions and many times even errors. The auditory approach had always been an alternative but was impossible to implement without working hearing aids and Phonic Ear units. Early print led to a nursery in which every item was labeled but to no improvement in reading scores. And American Sign Language, the natural language of deaf people, was not the natural language of the majority of their students, whose parents were hearing. Teachers had to teach American Sign Language to their students as a first language before they could teach them English as a second language.

The Fitzgerald Key, a method of filling in patterns of sentences, was for many years the chosen technique for teaching language. Children were taught lists of words categorized on charts that covered classroom walls from ceiling to floor, and then they wrote meaningful or meaningless but grammatically correct sentences. (who, verb, what, where, when: Mary brought boots to the lunchroom yesterday.) Teachers also wrote *experience* stories related to classroom happenings for and with their students. As the children progressed, they created their own independent compositions. Their daily "news" began with one sentence and over the years increased to a paragraph. This "news" might be an eyewitness account of a man shot in one of the children's projects the night before, or a sentence about how that boy or girl had watched TV again. Sadly, there was often no way of really knowing for sure if a man had been shot in their apartment building or on TV. Writing about a school event was preferable.

The current use of an Individual Education Plan required listing sequential behavioral objectives for language instruction. Each child in the class might be at a different developmental stage: communicating in one-word, two-word, or three-word sentences, asking questions, using subordinate clauses such as one beginning with *because.* Teachers had the task of moving students along to the next conversational step, always simultaneously evaluating their progress. (John will communicate in three-element sentences with 80% accuracy: "boy hit girl.")

Teachers used motherly natural language to model instruction.

"New shoes."

"Yes, Tony has new gym shoes. Mommy bought them yesterday. They cost a lot of money."

The teachers accepted language as it developed, constantly

communicating and waiting for their students to develop the same sequence of utterances as hearing children, only later, much later. They were willing to try any technique that had validity. They appreciated the children's small successes and were buoyed by them. One view they would never accept was that deaf children don't succeed because their teachers don't expect them to.

A teacher is what I want to be
And I will teach deaf children
How to write, do math problems
And what is right from wrong.
I will teach sign language and reading,
How to play new games and to dance,
To draw pictures I will hang on the wall.
I will be proud to be a teacher.

Jennifer, deaf

When we had the deaf children come to our school, I felt strange because I couldn't communicate with them.

Anna, seventh grade

Ms. Maureen Brownell was Kinzie's team leader, a teacher position endowed by the special education coordinators with supervisory responsibilities. Her job required, as she said, "wearing many hats." It involved making decisions on curriculum and materials, on placement of children, on multidisciplinary conference arrangements, on staff problems and in-service needs, as well as working in consort in all of these areas with Ms. May Werner, the assistant principal for the deaf department. Brownell was incredibly well suited to her job because there was no one more organized than she in the Chicago system. A sharpened pencil always protruded a bit from her professionally coifed blonde hair, and a panoply of messages was pinned to her purse. She lived by the code of color coordination, and it served her well. Newsletters were in the yellow folders, curricular materials in the blue, in-service in the green; every memorandum had its place in the rainbow. A frequent presence at educational conferences, she read the professional journals and shared articles on helpful teaching techniques with her co-workers.

Her room housed a wall of file cabinets containing duplicating masters for language, reading, math, social studies, science, and health and safety worksheets. Two long conference tables in the center of the room were surrounded by the largest collection of adult-size chairs in the building. That circumstance along with the semipermanent installation of the department 100-cup coffee pot made Brownell's room the formal and informal meeting place of the special ed staff. Birth announcements, graduate degrees, hospitalizations, and wakes were posted on her bulletin board. Teachers teased that she owned part interest in Weber's Bakery since she regularly cut up a coffee cake to celebrate some individual or group accomplishment. Sometimes coffee cake was a lure to the numerous meetings "our side" was always scheduling. Brownell had curriculum meetings; Werner, procedural meetings; Banks, speech meetings; and occasionally, Mr. Franklin held special informational meetings just for the teachers of deaf students. There were seasonal gatherings too, about assembly plans or departmental activities like the annual Thanksgiving feast.

On the Wednesday before the holiday each class who wished to do so prepared some festive food in supplies large enough to feed one hundred hungry deaf children and their teachers. Decked out as Indians or Pilgrims, they spread a Thanksgiving table in the lunchroom to complement the turkey plate served by the Board Food Services staff. There was homemade butter shaken by the preschoolers for the cornbread baked in some primary teacher's portable oven. Cranberries were mashed, sweet potatoes were smothered with marshmallows, stuffings were mixed with mystery ingredients, and a colorful spectrum of pumpkin pies were baked in hues from bright orange to gray-brown. Mr. Franklin, the consummate Pilgrim Father in a tall, black, construction-paper hat, bestowed his blessings at every class's table. And there was the large tepee on the stage decorated by the Cub Scouts.

Ms. Brownell had been mailed a brochure about scouting for the disabled from the Chicago Hearing Society, and she and Mary Daley attended the first year of meetings. Mary's girls were the prima ballerinas of the dance class, and she had been looking for a complementary esteem-building activity for her boys on those end-of-the-week, Friday-afternoon last periods of the day. Cub Scouts became the answer. Mary and Trudy, then Stan and Marilyn, and Flo and Gloria, and David and Ron (there was always a willing group of staff members) led the primary-age boys with disabilities through a variety of badge projects, from cleaning up the school grounds to attending the council hikes around the city.

> We went outside to dig. First we put flower food in the dirt. Then we dug holes with spoons. Last we put flowers in the holes. The flowers are pretty. The Cub Scouts put water on the flowers because water helps to make the flowers grow.
> The Cub Scouts picked up lots of garbage. Kinzie School looks nice and neat now.
>
> Keith, communication disorders class

Sign language also became one of Brownell's special interests, and she served as interpreter for Kinzie's two teacher aides who were deaf. She organized practice sessions in American Sign Language for the special ed teachers, who found learning ASL challenging because its grammar was so different from that of English. She invited the teacher aides, Barbara and Beth, to energize these classes with real-life ASL conversations.

Barbara also assisted Brownell with the weekly parent sign-language classes, which were taught in signed English. Whenever a parent enrolled his or her child in Kinzie's deaf program, the entire family was invited to participate in the Wednesday sign-language class. Teachers sent home regular reminders. Sometimes, there would be as many as twenty or thirty parents attending, other times only five or six. Sometimes, parents would concentrate on lists of vocabulary words, but other times Barbara would start a signed message at one end of the group and involve everyone in a game of "Rumors." The parents, at first, had hearty laughs at the surprise sentences that made their way around the circle. But as the weeks passed, the parents could congratulate themselves more frequently because they succeeded in communicating in sign language with one another.

Often, too, Barbara shared her personal experiences with the mothers, grandmothers, sisters, and occasional fathers, telling them stories about her own mom's misadventures with a deaf child. She related how she had lost her hearing when she was a baby. Her high fever had been broken by a powerful antibiotic that also caused her to become deaf. Barbara explained how difficult it had been for her to learn to speak, struggling to duplicate the sounds by sight and touch. She showed them her hearing aid and gave them tips on how to keep one in good working order. She demonstrated how to use a Telecommunication Device for the Deaf (TDD), telephoning her deaf friend and typing a message reminding her about their bowling league schedule.

On sign-class day parents were allowed to ride the school bus with their children if they had no other means of transportation. Some parents carpooled and brought their toddlers along. A bilingual mother translated for those who spoke only Spanish. The school nurse talked about immunization, nutrition, and medication. The social worker offered assistance with public agency forms and family conflicts. Ms. Brownell kept toys and games to occupy the preschoolers and always had a coffee cake on hand. Occasionally, a parent would bring home-baked chocolate chip cookies or crispy cinnamon buñuelos.

It was a warm and welcome cacophony of sign-language instruction in two languages simultaneously, counseling, scolding, nibbling, and chatting. The invisible bond of shared frustration was transformed into a visible network of coping strategies. Although a delicate thread, it provided the needed elasticity to support one Kinzie mother when her deaf child succumbed to a congenital heart defect. Aaron, just six years old and struggling with many health problems, seemed to have reached a plateau of stability, when an unexpected set-back sent him into the hospital for surgery. A frail boy with a weak heart, he did not survive the operation. Aaron's mother returned faithfully for many months to the sign language class where she found solace being with the other parents and teachers.

Brownell began sign-language classes for the teachers in the regular grades during the 8:30 to 9:00 morning preparation period. A hectic time in the day, this half hour often dwindled to a mere fifteen minutes. There were so many alternative ways to spend this time, even chatting with another teacher—sometimes a survival strategy—that the classes were sparsely attended. And the hearing teachers had no motivation, no contact with the deaf children.

Then Brownell began sign classes for the hearing children, twenty minutes a week of abc's, "Hello," "How are you?" "Fine," and hot, cold, good, bad, silly, fat, stop, and go, along with "The Star Spangled Banner" and "Jingle Bells." The regular classroom teachers had the freedom to decide if their entire class would participate or if a select group would attend, if sign class would be a privilege or a reward. It was a novelty. Ms. Brownell made it a fun time for all, and she sparked a deep new interest in a few children. But the regular students hadn't yet discovered sign language's enormous potential for long-distance classroom communication, freedom from getting caught whispering or passing notes.

Hearing brothers and sisters of the deaf students began to transfer into Kinzie, to board the same bus each morning instead of different ones. And they began learning how to communicate with their siblings.

I have a ten year old brother who is deaf. Michael loves to skate and work on his math. He enjoys playing with his stuffed animals. He is kind and friendly. Michael is great.

Michelle, fifth grade

To imagine is something we all do
To dream of a place that is just for you
Where people are kind and people care
Where people aren't selfish but try to share
It's nice to know that we can stay
For the arts can take us away every day.

Tara, seventh grade

I started organizing the deaf department assemblies back at Marquette School, probably because one of my speech classes always had a poem or skit memorized and ready to perform. I relied on the arts as a framework for my speech lessons. Special ed required innumerable repetitions, and having a hearing loss precluded picking up any information incidentally. The arts made repetition more palatable. Speech was conversation. Conversation was dialogue. Dialogue was high drama or low comedy. There was a sign on my room bulletin board, at the children's backs but facing me, that read, "The arts make man human."

That first Christmas at Kinzie, the deaf department had its annual holiday assembly on the Wednesday before vacation; assemblies were always on Wednesday, parent sign-class day. The audience was treated to dancing evergreen boughs in flowing, green tunic strips with snowy garlands in their hair. The littlest angels fidgeted with their bells and tambourines, some a beat ahead, some a beat behind, a few on time with their teachers, and some still waiting for the beat to start. The teachers on "our side" enjoyed putting on these little extravaganzas as much as their students enjoyed being center stage.

Although the teachers complained about the stressful preparation, and the kids worried about stage fright, the good spirits that bubbled up from these department efforts lasted almost until it was time to prepare another one.

The 1982 Christmas assembly took the theme of the traditional Bethlehem story. On stage next to the leaning cardboard stable stood three not-too-prosperous-looking kings with very royal smiles. A dozen raggedy shepherds hesitantly approached the manger. But the climax of the scene came, neither with the birth of Jesus nor with the arrival of the angels, but when Rommie, one of the shepherds, beckoned to his companions and said with a perfect *k* sound, "Come, come. The baby is born." This audience could appreciate his accomplishment, could understand the effort he had put into that speech.

Mr. Franklin concluded the program with a Christmas wish for the children. With a gentle waver in his voice he said, "Boys and girls, I hope that you get what you want for Christmas. I got my Christmas present early this year. It arrived when the deaf department came to Kinzie School."

Then Mr. Franklin asked me to arrange for the deaf children to present an encore performance for the hearing classes. After the second assembly many of the regular teachers commented how deeply they were touched by the program. And the hearing children expressed their wish that they could have been part of the assembly too.

Christmas is
a beautiful season
We all are together
for a special reason.

Rozanne, sixth grade

The following February, Ms. Mary Cutsworth, the fourth-grade teacher, created a multimedia assembly focusing on the children's idol of the time, E.T. Mary was one of the teachers forced to transfer into Kinzie as part of the desegregation initiatives. She was an artistic person—attractive, articulate, a poet and a teacher with a deep understanding of the emotions arising from being different. She chose for the protagonist of her program the Earth Stranger, who symbolized the two school populations unknown to each other till that year: the little wrinkled movie creature who phoned home, was at first feared, but became dearly loved by all of the children. Mary and I managed to produce a show that everyone could understand and enjoy, "We Love E.T." Hearing-impaired Olivia overcame her shyness and signed the welcome as Joanna recited it. Arturo's expressive face and sign-language rendition of "Someone in the Dark" evoked as much feeling as John's rich singing voice. Ms. Leemin interpreted the story in sign as the deaf and hearing children sitting in the magically darkened auditorium viewed the story slides created by the fourth-grade class for this special showing. *This was the first of the side-by-side assemblies.*

Then in May 1983, almost every room in the school came together to present *Kinzie Friends*. Classes teamed, a hearing with a deaf room, for the poem, "I Love People, All Kinds of People," and the songs, "Getting to Know You," "It's a Small World," and "The Greatest Love of All." Ms. Brownell was teaching the upper grades "I Hear Your Hand," an emotional musical plea for the acceptance of sign language. The parents were enthusiastically practicing the hit, "You've Got a Friend." And the dance class, now the size of the Rockettes but much less synchronized, was bouncing through its second partner dance to "Friends." I was coordinating *Kinzie Friends*, a program that read like friendship overkill. It was a collection of poems and songs deliberately selected by the teachers, yet it was a spontaneous expression of goodwill, the culmination of a year of experimental encounters.

Children were discovering for the first time that they were not all alike. Some of them could not hear, and some could not speak clearly. But they could communicate. They all could talk with their hands. Seeing children signing became a common experience. The hearing children were becoming comfortable with the signs of difference.

It still lay ahead for both groups to look beyond their differences and recognize their similarities.

June, 1983

Dear Parents and Friends of Kinzie School:

The many successes of this school year are directly attributable to the cooperative atmosphere that exists between the staff and parents. We confidently antici-pate the continuation of that spirit of sharing when school opens in September.

James P. Franklin

CHAPTER 8

On Funday in FIBruary,
The kids all jump and shout,
They all turn into clowns
And let their giddiness come out.

Rebecca, seventh grade

lbert asked the question first in speech class, on a balmy Indian summer day when shafts of sunlight highlighted the "sha(r), shaw, shoe, shee" on the speech chart and the warm-for-October breeze blew the playground noises into the classroom. It was recess time for the hearing children, and their songs and shouts were so exuberant that they bothered Albert. He was having a horrible time with the drill. What he finally managed to say was "Why me no outside play?"

And I rephrased his question to "Why can't I play outside?" but I didn't have the answer. "Only the hearing children have recess. The deaf children don't have recess" wasn't good enough. Albert knew the word *why*, and he knew *again*. And he could ask why again and again until somebody really thought about the answers instead of just giving them. The deaf children didn't have recess in the old school so they didn't have it here. No one included it in their schedule. Someone said it was for their own safety. No one was sure what the dangers were.

I told Albert to ask Mr. Franklin his question, and he did. Mr. Franklin looked deep into Albert's eyes, and said, "That's a good question. I think you should play outside." As a matter of fact, it was a question that had already become a kernel in the back of his own mind, waiting for some spark like Albert to ignite it.

And things started popping. A new schedule providing fifteen minutes for recess was typed up, the same fifteen minutes the hearing children had. Teachers on "our side" were given an outdoor duty schedule, compliments of Albert. Even the preschool children could play outside. Homer Price's donut bonanza, in which donuts popped out from a donut machine gone berserk and rolled everywhere , couldn't compete with the racing, pushing, tumbling, karate-chopping horde of one hundred deaf students that exploded out of the school doors and confronted the two teachers on duty, only one of whom knew sign language. Balls were intercepted, jump ropes snatched, unwanted tag games started, misunderstandings and miscommunications were everywhere on the playground. There had to be a better way.

A recess committee was formed. Marcia, who was a special ed teacher but also taught art until those positions were all closed, was enlisted to draw a diagram of the play area; and the committee, as seriously as the Axis powers, divided it into territories of domination. The deaf preschoolers and the hearing kindergarten got the swings and slides and teeter totters. The upper grades were assigned the farther-out playing fields, and the remainder of the play area was divided between primary and intermediate age children.

> We taught the six year olds to jump rope and play games. It was fun to watch and play with the deaf children.
> Kimberly, fifth grade

Playleader volunteers were chosen from the best signers in Ms. Brownell's hearing sign-language classes. Her philosophy of color coordination, which by now had permeated the school, was used to designate play groups. Play leaders had color sashes that were stored in a special locker. Colored geometric shapes were hung in the halls and painted on the grounds so that groups would line up in an orderly manner to exit and enter the building. The Parents Club provided money for equipment, playground balls, and jump ropes. A dedicated committee of teachers, Marcia, Marilyn, and David, volunteered to be consistent monitors of the program because recess duty was a shared responsibility, a week's duration. As soon as the two duty teachers became familiar with the routine, the guard changed.

Although recess had become more fun for everyone, it also became clear that a schoolwide deaf awareness program was needed. Primary hearing children thought their deaf playmates were starting fights, poking them in the back, when they were just trying to get their attention. Turn-taking often broke down when communication failed.

> We know what the deaf children are like. They're mean. They hit and push and steal and lie.
>
> Communication Arts Students

It was Mr. Franklin's suggestion that I write a proposal for a gifted program bringing the best deaf and the best hearing children together for the arts. It was an exciting way of integrating both groups on a regular basis, a challenging idea. I could reverse mainstream the brightest students first.

There were bright deaf students. There was Trina, a haiku poem, delicate in feeling, something lovely in nature. She didn't rhyme, but she had a regular rhythm. From the time she came to the nursery with her china-doll face, baby nose, and Buster Brown haircut, she was loved. The etiology of Trina's severe hearing loss was a mystery, but the broken elbow, the bumps and abrasions soon were explained. Teachers never had to remind Trina, as they did so many of the other happy-go-lucky preschoolers, to "Pay attention, watch me." She exhibited extraordinary concentration and a mature sad curiosity. They were evident in her glance, the slight movement backward, tilted head and raised eyebrow. She seemed so self-disciplined for a young child. No one knew she stood for long periods of time in the corner of her room. When the bruises were reported to Division of Children and Family Services (DCFS), Trina was whisked off to Hong Kong.

After a while she returned to the same abusive home environment and to Kinzie School. Nurtured in suffering, she was finally rescued by three successive Kinzie teachers who became her foster mothers when she most needed them. Freed at last, she developed excellent speech and speech-reading skills, and she found a release in the make-believe world of drama, art, and dance. When Trina was six years old, Brownell and I drove her to the Center on Deafness Creative Arts Festival, where she won third place for the Midwest Region in the dance competition. Later, she sparkled on the stage as Clara in the Nutcracker; she radiated as Mary in the Christmas story. She was bright, and in spite of all her personal adversity, she excelled.

And there were others. Ben's hearing loss was profound, his speech strained; but his language was excellent, and he had a solid speechreading foundation. With his curly blonde hair he was little boy blue, any mother's favorite son, a little shy but with smiling azure eyes under his long lashes. Ben was quiet but alert, a hard worker, self-directed, never distracted by the silliest antics of a classmate. And also Robert.

He had plenty to say, and most everybody could understand his speech with its natural, lilting black dialect. He was hard of hearing, according to his audiogram, but was placed in the deaf program because a past teacher had labeled him "hard of thinking." Robert's thoughts may have been traveling in a circuitous path, but they were certainly speeding along. Robert had questions about every topic. Olivia was shy, unbelievably shy, a fragile bud. For weeks she had refused to enter the preschool classroom, had to be gently coaxed over the threshhold. Even now she never volunteered, but you could tell when she knew the answers by the flush in her cheeks and the bright specks that appeared in the two dark pools of her eyes. Her hearing loss was moderate, but her hearing aid was usually without a battery or missing entirely. It was hard convincing her parents how much she needed it. Then they spoke only Spanish at home, and Olivia, only English in school.

The hearing girls first chosen for the gifted class were already members of dance, and they were beginning to become troupers: bouncy Joanna, athletic Lesley, artistic Tara, pensive Rebecca, amiable Jane, quiet Natalie, and intelligent Michelle. The arts class was new to the boys and not quite as appealing.

It was a pull-out program, and that involved some manipulation of schedules because students were still responsible for all of the regular work in their classrooms. Teachers who had to cover the curriculum and answer for their children's standardized test scores weren't eager to see students out of the room on a regular basis, and not specially for the arts. And I still had my speech classes as my primary responsibility. I was meeting weekly with the deaf department teachers about speech testing, objectives, and teaching techniques. Every month a different teacher from "our side" suggested a game, a worthwhile activity for reaching some speech goal. I saw to it that games were duplicated and distributed to all of the teachers of the deaf, and I continued to monitor children's personal and school hearing aids.

But this gifted class was original, tailored to the needs and strengths of Kinzie students. It looked good on paper: sign language, mime, rhythms, story dramatization, hearing science, art, music, and social studies related to drama. My grant read, "The Communication Arts Program will be presented in total communication and enable the gifted child to develop creative imagination, initiative, resourcefulness, freedom in bodily expression, growth in the enjoyment of good literature, appreciation for drama, and understanding of human differences, especially the disability of deafness."

There were sixteen in all, five of the brightest deaf students and eleven of the best hearing fourth and fifth graders. They were the same age but worlds apart in academic skills. The brightest hearing children were reading one or two grades above level, and the deaf children, with their above-average potential, still tested two or three grades below level.

We finally began in January of 1984. I met with the hearing children first, to offer some insights into the experience of living without sound. They said they knew what the deaf children were like. On the playground they had found out how the deaf kids hit and pushed and snatched and then denied doing those things.

They watched "Deaf Like Me," a thought-provoking video that presented the other side of their playground experiences. Yollie, the little deaf girl in the film, was most often left out of the recess games or treated as the butt of the hearing children's jokes. Then they listened to the unfair hearing test that simulated a mild hearing loss, and they attempted to puzzle out the auditory message when the most important pieces were missing. They were beginning to develop a little empathy. They tried on the Phonic Ear units, learned about the ear and how they hear and why the deaf children couldn't. They learned that the tiny sensory hair cells in the inner ear were destroyed and could never be repaired. They practiced a few basic conversational phrases in sign language. "What is your name? How old are you? What is your room number?" Some had difficulty with fingerspelling their names.

The first meeting was a get-acquainted party. Barbara Peters and I had made name tags with the I Love You hand sign. Barbara, who was teaming in the class, and I planned to pin them on backwards. When a deaf child and a hearing girl or boy could ask and answer the three questions of each other, they could turn their name tags around. The deaf children arrived first and took every other chair in the large circle. As the hearing children entered, Terry, with his best speech said, "The girl is fat!"

Blunt Terry had blundered us all into the real world, where judgments are made not only on the basis of skin color and disabilities but also on differences in weight, and hairstyle, and clothes. The fickle world where everybody is vulnerable. Terry knew only part of the real world. Because of his hearing loss, he had missed the spoken social nuances. He didn't absorb the ambience of politeness in which one person doesn't call attention to another's differences. But even subtler, Terry, along with all of the students in this class, had yet to discover the world in which one looks beyond those differences to a person's inner worth.

In the video "Deaf Like Me," Yollie develops confidence in herself when a mime visits her class, and after some self-doubt she succeeds in performing with him. Mime became the class introductory unit on drama, and it provided challenging activities in which both groups could achieve equally.

Ben had the best visual memory, and no one could surpass him in the Repeat-and-Add-On-a-Movement game, not even competitive Bryan. Brown-haired, brown-eyed and freckled, Bryan, who was *cool* in addition to being smart, was the natural leader of the hearing kids.

In the mime activities Kelven began with pulling a rope, and he was convincing. Joanna added creativity when she put a string on her hand. But Ben topped them all when he realistically wrapped the rope around himself and then gave it a tug. When Bryan marveled at Ben's ability, it set a tone of acceptance in the class.

I was lucky to get a professional mime through one of the city's few gifted programs arts residencies. The entire school was treated to a performance but the communication arts class was treated to a series of workshops. They culminated in a performance that included the moonwalk, the wall, and the rope to the hit song "Flash Dance." It was an assembly smash, and what was great was the kids created it together by themselves; they were the choreographers.

When it came to acting out plays, the language disparities necessitated selecting simple skits that first year. In the back of my file cabinet was a sacred bundle put in my trust, a yellowed folder of language plays that had been created by a teacher of deaf children "before my time." This teacher had believed in teaching language through little dramas of un-dramatic events. There was "Jane Goes Downtown," "Jane Buys a Blouse," and "Judy's Surprise Birthday Party." They were all short, one-scene plays that provided just the right amount of challenge because the hearing students had to sign as they spoke. I obtained a video camera for the school from a small-grants proposal, and Barbara videotaped the final per-formances.

Mr. Franklin was trapped during one of his routine visits

when the kids persuaded him to participate in their final production. He committed to being Dad, and he had three lines to learn in sign language. Although he was taking a night class in manual communication, he had been avoiding the first and most important step, actually fumbling into trying to communicate.

Mr. Franklin's dialogue was directed to Robert: "Help me clean the garage, and I will take you to McDonald's."

And later, "We came back at just the right time."

Robert: "In time for cake."

And there was a chocolate layer cake that the girls had baked and decorated with pink frosting and birthday candles, and pop and potato chips that the designated hearing and deaf children had brought, and balloons and streamers that were hung festively around the classroom as part of the drama. It was a genuine celebration. Real life mirrored their plays. They had become a group of friends, chatting and planning together, quibbling about details. They were no longer the deaf kids and the hearing kids, but the communication arts kids. And finally, just kids.

Communication Arts helped me realize the difficulties deaf people face in everyday life. It made me think about how I'd feel if I were deaf. When the deaf children first came to our school, I felt jealousy, resentment, and threatened that they would affect our school life and take over our school. Their coming did change the school, but not for the worse, for the better.

Tara, seventh grade

CHAPTER 9

Summer school is an ongoing direct service educational program for severely to profoundly handicapped children. As you know, sign-language classes for parents are not to be held in the schools during the summer session. For those parents who wish to take sign-language classes during the summer, they may contact Jane Blatt, coordinator, Deaf Programs and she will direct them to agencies offering classes.

I n June 1984, Mr. Franklin received a copy of a letter sent to Ms. Altschuler. It was signed by Fred Barnes, the director of Special Education, and cosigned by the assistant superintendent of Pupil Personnel Services and Special Education, the deputy superintendent of Field Management, and the deputy superintendent of Education Services. Mr. Franklin suspected that for some inexplicable reason this directive was an attempt to sabotage his program. Developing communication was the first priority for deaf students; parent participation in this process was fundamental. There was no rational justification for denying them this service one hour of the week. It wasn't likely that the director of Special Education would concern himself about one sign-language class in a school far out near the southwestern boundary of the district. Whatever the motivation, it most definitely was not a primary concern for the children's welfare.

Ms. Altschuler directed Mr. Franklin to follow the memorandum. She would not tolerate another parent letter-writing campaign. Besides, she and the director of special education went back a long way. Alice and Fred had been friends since their college days. She didn't want him bothered. The contact in the letter was Ms. Blatt. Fred had probably rubber-stamped it as a routine matter. Summer school lasted only six weeks. Mr. Franklin decided he might have to lose one skirmish in order to win the war.

With the new school year Communication Arts expanded to hearing students from second through sixth grade and bright deaf children of comparable ages. Scheduling became more complicated because more of the regular classes were affected. Some of the regular teachers were skeptical of the educational value of the communication arts program.

Only because Mr. Franklin supported these classes did the skeptics grudgingly relinquish their students, but they made their opinions known to the principal and in the teachers' lunchroom. In the past they had taught truly gifted students. Their artwork, their compositions, their reading and math scores and their science projects had been outstanding. The teachers hadn't seen assignments of comparable quality in years. Now, more than half of Kinzie's students were eligible for free lunches. The school's racial composition had shifted to approximately 40 percent white, 40 percent black, and 20 percent Latino. The regular teachers quipped that a goodly number of their students could probably profit from special tutoring instead of a gifted program. And what they observed of the deaf students confirmed their convictions that the special education students would never be appropriately placed in their own classrooms. It was up to me to justify these interruptions to the basic curriculum.

My youngest speech classes were now delegated to two of the preschool teachers, but I continued to teach all of the primary students. I was working with reverse mainstreamed classes part-time. Ms. Brownell was teaching sign-language classes to the regular grades 160 minutes a week.

Ms. Blatt requested a conference with Mr. Franklin about

the utilization of Kinzie's special education staff in programs that included hearing children. At their meeting she pointed out that special education teachers were paid to instruct only special education students. She reiterated that special education was a separate entity, totally divorced from regular education. She emphasized the word *separate*. And she reminded Mr. Franklin that special education's funding mandated provision of services to *handicapped children*. The implication was that including regular students in classes taught by special education personnel was illegal.

The coordinator further explained that one deaf department position had been allotted specifically for group speech, in order to provide each class with additional instruction in speech, speechreading, and auditory training. Mr. Franklin countered that he had scrutinized the hearing-impaired program when it transferred to his school. He found that at various times, this class had focused on group auditory training, art, and even an amorphous blend of home economics and science. It was a program designed primarily to give teachers of the deaf their third preparation period each week. Its concomitant objective was to provide *some* profitable educational experience for the children.

In addition, this speech position was a subterfuge, not an exception, not *nonquota*. Every Kinzie teacher of deaf children was *quota*. They were all counted in determining the special education teacher/pupil ratio. It could very well be that with a few more enrollments, the departmental speech class would have to be terminated and its teacher assigned to a self-contained division. If Ms. Blatt wanted a position categorized as group speech, she should obtain a nonquota number for another teacher.

Furthermore, Mr. Franklin quoted section 6–12 of the Rules of the Chicago Board of Education:

Principals of schools are the responsible administrative heads of their respective schools and are charged with the organization, supervision, administration, and discipline thereof. They shall establish and enforce such regulations, not contrary to the Rules of the Board of Education or the regulations of the General Superintendent of Schools, as in their judgment may be necessary for the successful conduct of their schools.

Ms. Blatt argued that because of her training and experience, she was the specialist most able to decide what was best for deaf children. She was most qualified to determine the use of special ed staff members. Ms. Blatt decreed that the organization most beneficial to the students at Kinzie was assigning Ms. Banks to teach only the group speech classes to the deaf children. Mr. Franklin's stubborn insistence on organizing his own school prompted Ms. Blatt to recite sarcastically what was becoming one of her most frequently quoted poems:

You will be convinceable
Because I am invincible.
God made me principal!

At the conclusion of their meeting, she stated ominously that Mr. Franklin left her no alternative but to "take pen in hand."

During the next districtwide special education in-service for teachers of deaf children, Ms. Blatt announced that some Chicago schools were developing luxury programs and depriving students of the basics. Inferring an analogy to the communication arts class, she declared that a fur coat is nice, but the Chicago system is in the market only for cloth coats. She stated that Mr. Barnes, the Director of Special Education, had expressed his concern that deaf kids weren't talking any more. Their teachers were not teaching speech.

Jane Blatt should have known better. She was one of "our side" gone up the ladder. As a teacher of the deaf, her major priority had not been speech, but she knew it was taught. Her own curriculum specialty had been science. Teachers often traded their students to her for units in biology or astronomy; in return, they taught her students speech. Because the Chicago Board of Education continued to be entrenched in a philosophy of strictly oral communication, Jane became one of the first advocates for manual communication. Fingerspelling was one of her special competencies. Her hands unobtrusively and incessantly shifted from one letter of the alphabet to another. As colleagues smoked or chewed gum in the teachers' lounge, Jane fingerspelled. Even before the policy shift to total communication, Jane amazed everyone with her fluency, fingerspelling entire songs, never missing even a preposition.

At Marquette School she was spontaneously acknowledged as the department disciplinarian; everyone admired the behavior of her children's lines in the halls and at the door. Cooly, she dismissed an entire wing without even the regular troublemakers acting out. Her name sign, which was the index finger pointing to the nose, had the connotation of *mean,* don't mess with her. She was respected.

Jane taught college-level special-education classes. She was one of the early supporters of the state organization of the Illinois Teachers of the Hearing Impaired. At the initiation of Public Law 94–142, she had been forced to defend the board of education in numerous due process hearings, to take an adversarial position against powerful education advocates like Senator Berman, who had proposed the legislation. Jane had once defended my nursery program against a parent who filed for tuition reimbursement for private school placement. The father, who had never even been in the school, testified that he wouldn't send a dog to the classroom. His wife had registered their daughter in the public school program while they were waiting for her acceptance into a parochial school. They intended to transfer her as soon as her name moved up the waiting list. But it occurred to them that they might make the Chicago Public Schools pay their daughter's tuition if they could prove that the city nursery didn't meet her unique needs. The parents lost their case.

The case was symptomatic, however, of the board's major problem, overcoming its own bureaucracy. My orientation-clinic class had been developed with an excellent team teacher, and we were recognized for providing entering children with whatever support services they needed. City teachers, like us, in good programs, wasted hours away from our students and endured days of due-process hearings because the board failed to meet its deadlines, failed to distribute compulsory forms to its staff, and failed to in-service personnel on how to complete the forms. The due-process decision had vindicated our educational program, but the board had been directed to accelerate its delivery of special education services or face serious consequences in the future.

Ms. Blatt's days now were spent in placing handicapped children and overseeing multidisciplinary staffing matters. She worked most closely with Ms. Werner, Kinzie's assistant principal for the deaf department, but she rarely had time any longer to visit the program.

I was upset with Jane because of her characterization of

teachers of the deaf at the recent in-service meeting. Jane had attributed the criticisms to the director of special education, but it was doubtful that Mr. Barnes was concerned or even aware of how deaf kids were talking. He never visited the schools. Nevertheless, I wrote to Jane in response to the situation as she described it.

Dear Jane,

I was very disheartened by Mr. Barnes' remark that deaf kids don't talk any more and the following inference that this is the result of teachers of deaf children not teaching speech.

Last year the Kinzie Staff and I personally, as department speech teacher, expended a tremendous amount of time, energy, and effort in developing a viable department speech program based on the Chicago Speech Curriculum. We met by level at least once each month, often twice, to discuss evaluation techniques, to develop innovative speech games for our younger children and to establish a workable lesson format.

Most of our staff attended speech workshops on their own time; some actually took a course.

We selected a universal evaluative device, Ling's Speech Evaluation, and all of our teachers administered it to all of our students. I prepared in-services on this test and special help was offered to teachers who needed it.

Following evaluation, I provided short-term objectives correlating to the Chicago Speech Curriculum to teachers at all levels within our school. This made individualization yet continuity of instruction possible. And it facilitated IEP preparation.

Each month a different Kinzie teacher prepared a specific speech game or tool to share with the rest of the staff. I made multiples of these games for teachers requesting them.

Working in committee, we developed a practical format for formal group speech instruction. We also determined when it might be feasible to emphasize individual speech skills during the routine school day. I synthesized this format and provided in-services to the total staff. (copy enclosed)

Mr. Barnes is cognizant, I'm sure, of the changes in etiology of the typical deaf student in our classes today. Because we are aware of this diminishing speech potential, we at Kinzie have expended extra effort and energy on speech development to make our program genuinely one of total communication. I am very proud of what we have accomplished at Kinzie School in only one year, and I'd be happy to share this good news with Mr. Barnes at any time.

In March of 1985 I did a presentation at the annual conference of the Illinois Teachers of the Hearing Impaired (ITHI) on "Mainstreaming the Arts." It was a demonstration of the arts initiatives at Kinzie including the dance class, the Communication Arts program, and the assemblies I had arranged.

The assemblies had been selected on the basis of their suitability for a combined hearing and deaf audience and their cost. In a school system that had no money for repair of Phonic Ear auditory-training units, one couldn't expect funds to be allocated for the arts. Art teachers in Chicago's elementary schools were ancient history. I took the only avenue left to educators who believe that the arts should be a part of their students' experience—begging. I began to write letters and to apply for grants.

At home, after the last load of laundry came out of the dryer, four lunches were bagged, Lisa's creme puffs made for French class, Kris's neon socks found, Rachel's Indian report edited, and "The Very Hungry Caterpillar" read to Max, I settled down to my Apple IIC computer and composed one letter that could be sent to several businesses and one proposal that could be mailed to a few funding agencies.

Meanwhile, classes continued. The dance class girls had never seen a real ballet, never had the experience of "Swan Lake" to define the concept "graceful." Ticket costs and evening performance times made a ballet field trip out of the question so I wrote a letter. In return the Kinzie dancers received an invitation to the studio of the Chicago City Ballet. They curled up right under the barre as Paul Mejia, the director of the company, taught the full ensemble a practice class. The girls were so close to the dancers they could feel the perspiration in the air, see it bead on the dancers' foreheads, drip into their straining eyes, and soak through their leotards. It was a close up, inside look at dance and showed how much discipline, hard work, and practice were required to create the illusion of ease. Afterwards, the students mingled with the professionals, asking questions, collecting their autographs. Back at school we made a special bulletin board about "our" Chicago City Ballet, and the girls resolved to point their own toes a little harder and kick a little higher.

And then the ballet came to Kinzie, thanks to a grant from the Illinois Arts Council and to donations from some local businesses and the Parents Club. Raising a thousand dollars was a formidable task, but Mr. Franklin predicted we could do it. The performance was scheduled for the seven-hundred seat auditorium of Kennedy High School next door so their senior drama students, dance classes, pompons, and cheerleaders were included among the audience. The community was invited, and children from a neighboring school attended; the hall was packed. Following the demonstration of exercises at the barre, which even involved some Kinzie students, the company performed selections from "Rodeo." It was a perfect choice, with its graceful girls and robust cowboys in exuberant combinations. Even the janitors commented upon how much they enjoyed the program, and parents and children who had never seen professional ballet before were enthralled. The dance-class girls had made roses in communication arts class and presented one to each dancer. The denouement to the afternoon's program was one of the high school cheerleader's fainting in the main hall when a cowboy tossed her his rose.

Some
people
soar through the
air like birds in
flight.

Mark, fifth grade

Thea Nerissa Barnes, a Chicago public school graduate and soloist with the Martha Graham Dance Company, came to Kinzie. She volunteered to teach a modern dance class and gave a breathtaking performance as Joan of Arc. A brass quintet of the Chicago Symphony Orchestra performed in the Kinzie gym. Art Resources for Teachers (A.R.T.), an organization attempting to compensate for the lack of art classes in Chicago's elementary schools, worked with children in grades five through eight, presenting sessions on sculpture, painting, photography, and architecture. The Clemente Steel Band entertained the school. All of these programs were free.

Dear Clemente Steel Band,
    We enjoyed your music. You let me play the drums. Thank you very much. I will play the drums next time when you come back another day. O.K.?
                                            Your friend,
                                            Robert, hard of hearing

And there was the new school newspaper, the *Kaleidoscope*. Ms. Peters and Ms. Kasper, Parents Club officers, rolled out the ancient, temperamental corn-popping machine and sold small bags of popcorn during the lunch periods. Proceeds from these sales paid for the printing of the Kinzie newspaper.

Every third Friday is Popcorn Day. We may ask mom my or daddy to have twenty-five cents for popcorn. We must use a good sentence like this, "May I have twenty-five cents for popcorn please?" Two ladies come to school and make popcorn for the children. The ladies put in the popcorn, salt, and butter. It tastes delicious! It smells good too.
                                            Trina, deaf

Exceptional Children's Week
May 5–11, 1985
Annually, the first week in May is designated "Exceptional Children's Week." Since more than one/fourth of our school population is deaf, we have planned some awareness activities for the entire school.

Our theme is "Free to be you and me." Throughout the week we will be selling buttons for fifty cents.

Marcia created several button designs, and the committee selected a deaf boy and a hearing girl signing "friends." A friend of a friend owned a buttonmaker which he loaned to Kinzie. The round, pink symbols of acceptance were worn proudly by the primary children, displayed less flamboyantly by intermediate students, and pinned indifferently to belts or inside pockets by upper-grade students.

We will be developing a mural outside the lunchroom. Individual figures will be drawn in the classroom and assembled by the mural committee. Please see Jackie Sothey in 107 to sign up for a category: children, clouds, insects, large or small animals, trees, plants, buildings, transportation. You can sign up beginning *today*.

Every classroom contributed. Their drawings were assimilated into a four-by-eight-foot collage of carefree deaf and hearing boys and girls, inhabitants of a cloudless town where a huge, red school towered over pastel-colored buildings and smiled on a vast, green park where all of the children played harmoniously in the midst of flowering trees, friendly animals, and blue birds in flight. After much deliberation the committee arrived at a consensus, and the cooperative masterpiece was mounted on a plywood panel and ceremoniously hung next to the lunchroom entrance, where every day the students could identify their parts of the total Kinzie picture.

Teachers of deaf classes can pair with teachers of regular classes for lunch and games on Monday, Thursday, or Friday. These plans can be made by teachers.

Mary Cutsworth and Marilyn Steiner shared more than lunch; they exchanged classes. Ms. Cutsworth spent the afternoon in the primary deaf classroom and Ms. Steiner taught third grade. Their shared insights led to a collegiality that lasted through the years and a variety of cooperative activities for their pupils in math, science, and the arts.

Lois Janus and Juanita Dornes joined their classes for games. It was exciting for Lois's class to play London Bridge and Farmer in the Dell with thirty other children instead of seven. The number of possibilities for a friend was overwhelming.

Four classes had a baseball game out on the high school's diamond. It was big-league competition for the primary communication-disorders class, the fourth graders, and two deaf rooms. Everyone went wild when the coaches came up to bat.

Kindergarten and Ms. Acento's deaf five-year-olds shared a quiet story hour reading of *Lisa In Her Deaf World,* followed by cookies and milk.

Marcia teamed her preschool deaf children with Ms. Brewer's fifth-grade class. After they shared lunch, together they planted petunias in the flower beds next to the main entrance of the school building. Ms. Brewer acquired a special helper, Brenton, the thorn in the side of every teacher who'd survived him, the terror of every child who'd stood next to him in line. For all his future years at Kinzie and for no reason that anyone could fathom, Brenton would find a respite from his tantrums in Ms. Brewer's class; she was the one teacher who momentarily calmed the tornadoes whirling inside him.

Ms. Brewer's students became room helpers in Marcia's and in other preschool classrooms. They helped with schoolbags and notes at dismissal, with snowsuits and boots in winter. They escorted a little boy or girl to the washroom, stapled papers, straightened chairs, and washed blackboards.

When the fifth graders were studying bees, Marcia, in full beekeeper attire, provided them with personal tips from her firsthand experience.

> Ms. Marcia Midler is a good beekeeper. I enjoyed her and her class being here with us. She told me sometimes when I see a wasp I will call it a bee. Today when she was here I saw two bees and a wasp. They look a little different and act differently. The wasp likes meat and they are mean. The bees are more friendly.
>
> Keayea, fifth grade

Regular students were given a writing exercise, defining "what *exceptional* means to me." The pupils were asked to describe an exceptional person they knew personally or one they had read about.

To me the word exceptional means someone or something that is extraordinary in some way. There is someone in my family who is an exceptional person to me. He is my dad, and he has a pacemaker.

Rebecca, third grade

Franklin Roosevelt was a president of the United States. In 1921 he became a polio victim. Because of this experience, he opened a clinic in the South for other people who had polio. There they learned to walk again. Mr. Roosevelt never got all of his strength back. Yet he was an exceptional president and an exceptional person.

Mark, fifth grade

Stevie Wonder is a popular singer. Even though he is blind, he has a nice voice and a lot of talent. He has written many popular songs. He has performed in concerts. His latest song is about sending food to the Ethiopians, "We Are the Children of the World." Stevie Wonder is blind but he can sing really well, and he cares about others.

Melvin, fifth grade

The communication arts students wrote compositions about deaf people with varied accomplishments. Ten students, two each day, were chosen to read their two-minute reports over the public address system to the entire school. Some of the regular teachers complained about the five minute interruption to their class activities, but only the few hard cases.

> During the past two days children have reported on a deaf man who is one of the best teachers in California, a deaf woman who acts in the National Theater of the Deaf, Kitty O'Neil whom you have probably seen in exciting stunts in movies and on TV, and a deaf girl your own age who will be on the Olympic ski team. It is not important to remember the names of these people but to learn that deaf people are successful in a variety of ways. The deaf children in our school have a difficult time learning to speak and read, but they can grow up to do work that is helpful to all of us, like Ms. Barbara Peters and Ms. Beth Sharp here at Kinzie.

There were nine hearing children chosen to speak on the intercom, and Robert. Robert's teachers rated his speech very intelligible, and just about everyone listened to him practice and gave him suggestions. Robert, who was usually bold enough, was getting very nervous about this project. He had experienced plenty of failures in the past; that was why he had been moved from hard of hearing to deaf placement. When he excitedly rushed through his lines, his speech would slur into a gibberish even his teachers couldn't translate. When he was calm and spoke slowly, he was clear enough. Chances were fifty-fifty that he would be understood.

> Fred Schreiber said, "I am deaf, but I am not trying to be a hearing person. I accept my handicap. Ears are not important. Brains are!"

Fred thinks deaf people should join clubs. Deaf children can join scouts.

Deaf grown-ups can join the N.A.D. [National Association of the Deaf]. Fred works hard for the N.A.D.

He travels and gives speeches. He is working to make a universal sign language. Then people all around the world could use the same signs.

If a deaf person from France met a deaf person from America, they could use the same signs. It is hard to get people from all over the world to agree on a universal sign language. But Fred is trying. He wants deaf people to know each other better.

Teachers:

Please copy the above on your blackboard this morning. It will be read over the intercom at 9:15 by a hard of hearing student, and we would like your class to read along silently as it is read aloud.

J. Franklin

The children read with their eyes as Robert read with his heart. He spoke slowly over the intercom, distinctly enough for almost everybody to understand. A spontaneous whoop of applause rang out through the school in all but a few classrooms. You could hear the second wave beginning a few seconds later in the rooms of the hard cases. Success is contagious. Congratulations poured in on Robert, enabling him to bounce along on a cushion of self-confidence for weeks. Robert was so impressed with himself that he worked hard enough to return to a hard of hearing class the following September.

Exceptional children are special because they are different in a way. Just because they are different in a way doesn't mean they can't do anything. Just because they are different in a way doesn't mean we don't care for them.

Edward, fifth grade

Ms. Blatt had attended my presentation at ITHI. During Exceptional Children's Week she requested a conference with Mr. Franklin. At that meeting she stated that it was imperative that I discontinue my mainstream activities and serve exclusively as "the designated teacher of speech," seeing children individually or in small groups. If I didn't assume this role, she demanded that I be assigned to a self-contained class.

Mr. Franklin reminded Ms. Blatt that I was still teaching on a self-contained classroom number. He had not received any nonquota position numbers so he would not be making any "designations." He reiterated that as the building principal he would decide my responsibilities within the Kinzie School program, just as he determined all other teachers' responsibilities within his program.

This flat refusal so angered Ms. Blatt that she heatedly blurted out, "Kinzie may be your school, but this special education program is mine!"

Mr. Franklin replied emphatically, "No, this program is mine, all mine."

The following month Mr. Franklin and Ms. Altschuler received the first of the "acquisition-of-speech" letters.

> Acquisition of speech for a deaf child is paramount if he/she is to function independently as a member of so-

ciety at large as an adult. Prerequisites for development of speech in deaf children are effective teaching and adequate opportunity. Adequate opportunity must be provided to exploit the conditions that contribute to the mastery of speech. A consistent sequential ongoing speech program and a sound educational approach to speech development is essential. A sound educational approach means programming children individually or in small groups based on diagnostic speech-and-language evaluations. To this end one teaching position in each deaf center has been allocated for a speech program.

Individualized speech training provided by the speech teacher would give the classroom teacher speech goals, isolated target sound, speech drills and speech specific to individualized needs. A truly integrated speech program is coordinated by the speech teacher.

There truly is no speech program at Kinzie School. Instead, we have two teachers giving speech to classrooms as a whole to provide preparation periods. At Kinzie School the speech teacher's time is now directed toward a Communication Arts Program. An excellent program, but not a speech program. It would be nice if the Communication Arts Program could continue, but to deprive the young deaf children of speech is to destroy the essence of their educational program. As stated earlier, speech is their door to the hearing world.

The children and I are looking forward to the development of a strong and viable speech program next fall.

Frances Woods, Director,
Bureau of Physically Handicapped Children
approved by Fred Barnes,
Director of Bureau of Special Education

Upon receipt of the letter, Mr. Franklin asked Ms. Altschuler to clarify the number of teaching positions in the deaf program, to obtain documentation for the provision of quota and nonquota teachers. He made copies of the time-distribution schedules of all of his special education personnel available to her.

More than anything else, Ms. Altschuler was aggravated by the possibility that some teacher might be floating around a school building, wasting time in some fluff program, seeing children one or two at a time. She was suspicious of support people. She believed that "real" education occurred when teachers were in their rooms, doors closed, children in their seats, teachers lecturing. She didn't understand small groups, individual instruction, or teaming. I, to her satisfaction, had a filled schedule of full-size classes.

In addition, Ms. Altschuler believed in following the *Rules of the Board of Education,* especially as they applied to the supremacy of *line* over *staff* positions. Principals and superintendents were *line*, coordinators and directors: *staff.* Staff people coordinated and assisted the line people who were in charge. The *Rules* stated that school organization was the principal's domain. Ms. Altschuler concurred. She readily arranged a meeting with Ms. Woods, who was the author of the letter and Ms. Blatt's superior. A summer summit was arranged in the District 18 office, Ms. Altschuler's turf, and it resulted in three agreements: First, the organization and utilization of staff at Kinzie was to be determined by Mr. Franklin. Ms. Woods had been an elementary school principal prior to her appointment to the administration, located on Pershing Road. She was cognizant of the board rules and apparently willing to abide by them. Second, Ms. Woods said she would wait for a call from Mr. Franklin if there were problems at Kinzie. She would not be writing any more letters such as the epistle on the acquisition of speech. Third, Ms. Woods agreed that Ms. Blatt would have to learn the appropriate role of the coordinator, which was to provide assistance to the school, not to be the principal in absentia.

At this meeting Mr. Franklin felt they had finally come to a determination that he was the administrator of Kinzie School, that he had the right to organize his teachers in the way he knew would most benefit all of his students. Therefore, he indicated that he was planning to substitute a group library program for the group speech classes for the deaf children. Neither Ms. Altschuler nor Ms. Woods objected. In addition, because the matter of the designated teacher of speech was resolved, Mr. Franklin introduced the topic of a genuine need for the services of a speech therapist for those deaf students who had the most residual hearing and who had identifiable speech deficiencies that could be remediated. His remarks were noted but received no comments.

In September 1985, I changed from group speech to group library. I teamed with Violet Benning, the school librarian. We developed a format for reading and signing stories together, reinforcing them with a filmstrip if possible, dramatizing the stories using the big box of leftover assembly costumes (Violet and I first, then the kids), and writing group or individual book reports with the deaf children. Violet had been teaching library for many years and had not done anything as crazy as these dramatizations in her entire previous career; but she saw that the deaf children were more able to understand the stories through a simple acting out of the plots, and she was a good sport. Violet began to learn signs and communicate with the deaf students. She checked to see that they had working hearing aids and reminded them to use their voices during the playlets. Violet and I were taking the first step to integrating library instruction, providing the deaf students with a foundation of library skills and developing a program that would be meaningful for *all* the students.

> This story is about the five Chinese brothers.
> The Chinese brothers all looked alike.
> The Chinese brothers all lived near the sea.
> The five Chinese brothers all had magic.
>
> Oralia, deaf

Then Ms. Quintain, the fourth-grade teacher, took an initiative. Motivated by her girls' participation in the dance class, she had them do large pastel drawings of ballet dancers in classic costumes. She sent these beautiful ballet portraits inspired by the works of Degas down to fill the walls of my classroom. It was a renaissance project for Ms. Quintain, for she had done exciting arts activities in the past when there were many capable students. Ms. Quintain was a no-nonsense teacher, but she had the artistic touch. Her students frequently prepared exquisite decorations for the main office doors, welcoming school visitors with bits of beauty.

Through serendipity and their Degas unit, the communication arts students became involved in an art project that culminated in a student exhibit at the Art Institute. Even Ms. Altschuler attended this reception. After three years of invitations to festivals and performances downtown, at Kinzie or at Kennedy next door, she finally got a firsthand look at their activities.

The project, called Cultural Exchange Through Art for Children, was funded through a proposal to the State Department of Education. Students from Kinzie, from Hinsdale, Illinois, and from Paris, France, viewed the exhibit "A Day in the

Country" and used their computers to complete a data base, to describe personal interpretations of the impressionist paintings, and to compose poems. The students also wrote one another letters and exchanged photographs. Then the Hinsdale students came to Kinzie with a treasure of art supplies, and together, the students created their own impressionist paintings using acrylics. The Junior Museum of the Chicago Art Institute exhibited their works. Kinzie parents, teachers, and administrators celebrated with the students at their opening-night reception.

In the gifted communication arts class, we are being prepared for the world. By communicating with deaf children, with people in other countries, and each other, we can have friends everywhere. I now realize what a big world there is yet to discover, so many people, so many places, and all the stories to hear.

The past years in the gifted program have been a rewarding experience. I have had the opportunity to see and learn a variety of things in the fields of art and literature.

First of all, we have seen dancers, plays, sculptures, and artwork, all performed or created by a variety of professionals.

Second, we learned how to communicate with deaf people through sign language. As any other language or subject, it takes practice to master it. We also learned a little about another language when we sent letters to children in France. We enjoyed finding differences and similarities in our countries, languages, and customs.

Our gifted program also has its own newspaper, the *Kaleidoscope*. We can interview our teachers and staff members of our school. We write poems, create cartoons, and we also report on current events in school.

I think all of these things someday will benefit us for our jobs or leisure, perhaps as dancers, actors and actresses, artists, teachers of deaf children, reporters, or computer programmers.

Now that we are involved in the gifted program, we'll never be the same. We have learned to develop skills we didn't know we had. We know we can set goals and reach them. We can become whatever we want to be.

Rebecca, seventh grade

CHAPTER 12

About one-third of Kinzie's deaf students were now learning with hearing children in communication arts or one of the mainstreamed arts classes taught by Marcia and me together. These students were also mainstreamed for library weekly. Violet and I were team teaching again to insure that stories chosen and seatwork selected were appropriate for both groups and that activities promoted genuine interaction between them.

One-half of the deaf population was mainstreamed for gym; child welfare attendants, who regularly attended the parent sign-class, interpreted game rules and instructions in the gym. It was impossible to mainstream all of the deaf classes because many were preschoolers and most were primary groups. The hundred-plus deaf children were all in the age range of three through eleven. Kinzie housed only one regular class of each grade. With the number of students in every grade in the thirties, the regular classes were too large to include more than one special ed class each. Therefore, some deaf children received all of their instruction in the self-contained special education classes. For one child this proved to be the "least-restrictive environment" called for by federal law P.L. 94–142 that his family had to fight for.

Edward is an eight-year-old, physically handicapped black male. He has encephalopathy, spastic dipligia, and a sloping, moderate-to-profound bilateral sensorineural hearing loss.

Edward looked different from the other Kinzie students who were deaf. He had trouble walking up and down the stairs. He had trouble writing and signing. It was the cerebral palsy. His hearing aids helped a lot, and he could imitate sounds well. He had trouble remembering the sounds. It was his slow rate of learning. He got along well with the other children. It was his wonderful disposition.

Edward was placed in a beginning primary classroom. He had difficulty carrying, cutting, zipper opening, closing, pouring, jumping, catching, standing on one foot, but he persisted. He carried his own tray in the lunchroom. His class was assigned the table closest to the lunch counter. He improved on the stairs. His teacher walked behind him on the way up and in front of him on the way down.

Sometimes he attempted to socialize with classmates by running headlong into them, slapping or pushing, but it was clear that he never meant to hurt them. He just wanted their attention. His classmates became accepting of him; he became more restrained in his greetings. Edward became a Cub Scout just like the other primary boys. The other children understood his problems. On the day of the hike in the woods, the children watched out for him. Most of them noticed numerous deep holes on the grounds. Every time they approached one, they all pointed and signed to Edward, "Look, *look!*" and "Be careful." Edward never fell in a hole. The only person who did was his teacher–scout leader, David, who was so busy watching Edward that he landed up to his knee in a muddy crevice himself.

Edward learned to communicate in statements consisting

of one or two signs. Career Awareness Day was an exciting time for Edward. His dad, a Chicago policeman who was stationed on a police boat in Lake Michigan, came to school in full uniform with all of his equipment. At his station in the gym, he spoke to small groups of Kinzie students about being a policeman. Some of the children tried on his hip boots and his wet suit. Edward signed to the other children, "Father Father. Policeman my," and they were impressed. You could see the admiration in Darius's eyes and the pride in Edward's.

In the fall of 1986, Edward's parents met with Ms. Werner in a pre–IEP conference to discuss his special needs. Mr. and Mrs. Washington were satisfied with the short- and long-term goals presented and with the services listed. In December they came back to Kinzie for a staffing—a multidisciplinary conference required by law that is held to determine a child's eligibility for services—that they thought would formalize their previous agreement and document it for school records. Instead, Ms. Blatt recommended that Edward's placement be changed.

Edward's parents perceived him to be hearing impaired, language delayed, and physically handicapped, in that order of significance to his academic development. They thought the professionals agreed. But, in the wake of reports from the speech and language pathologist, the school nurse, the clinical audiologist, the occupational therapist, the physical therapist, the classroom teacher, the itinerant teacher of the physically handicapped, the social worker, and the psychologist, Edward was described as primary: physically handicapped, secondary: hearing disabled. Therefore, Edward would have to transfer to Spalding School. The parents strongly objected, but the meeting was closed at the ring of the school bell.

The Washingtons immediately wrote a letter to the General Superintendent expressing their desire to have Edward remain at Kinzie in his current educational program. They stated that his impending transfer left them no alternative but to request a due-process hearing.

On February 13, Ms. Blatt asked Mr. Franklin to write a letter requesting a due-process hearing. He replied that he would have to review the case first. She stated that Edward needed a change in placement for increased physical therapy (Mr. Franklin did not find this recommendation made in the physical therapist's report.). She suggested that Edward might regress (Mr. Franklin found no supportive evidence for this observation in any of the reports.). She mentioned that Edward might need a communication board, a device where a student presses letters or code words to communicate (Mr. Franklin noted that reports by the communication specialists indicated Edward was making good progress with sign language.).

Resource Physically Handicapped Itinerant Teacher Report:

During the past year, Edward has shown marked improvement in his ability to function independently within the school setting. He is able to walk around the building, carry his own tray, and dress independently.

He attempts to vocalize and sign to communicate with me when I enter his room. He did not do this when he initially entered Kinzie School. He also, now, is able to walk quickly down the middle of the hall without touching walls or lockers for support.

On 14 February, Mr. Franklin called Mr. Washington and learned that he had enrolled Edward in a program for physical therapy twice a week and occupational therapy once a week at Christ Hospital. Mr. Washington reiterated his wish to have Edward continue at Kinzie School.

On 17 February, Mr. Franklin met with some of the staffing team and requested that they reconvene on 10 March to reconsider changing Edward's designation of handicaps, based on a closer examination of the individual evaluations and recommendations and on the additional information that Edward had been recently enrolled in programs at Christ Hospital.

On 18 February, Ms. Blatt informed Mr. Franklin that Frances Woods and a representative from the due process office would be present on 10 March. Mr. Franklin called the due process office and was assured that they would hold off pending results of the 10 March meeting.

On 23 February, Mr. Franklin spoke with the principal of Spalding School. She was emphatic in her judgment that Edward should not be placed at Spalding, a segregated setting and the "most restrictive environment." The program for Edward had five students; two were severely burned, profoundly deaf, and confined to wheelchairs, two were quadriplegics, and the fifth was a new child she didn't have information on yet. No student in the class was mobile; none could move anywhere without one-to-one assistance. Spalding's principal said that Edward was the kind of student she regularly attempted to have moved out of Spalding through multidisciplinary conferences. She further said that if Edward were sent to Spalding, she would request a due process hearing on the basis that the law requires the "least-restrictive environment." She offered to write a letter to the staffing team stating her views and objections.

On 3 March, Mr. Franklin visited Spalding and saw that there was only one deaf class in the school, and the only other person to sign besides the classroom teacher was the library teacher.

On 4 March, Mr. Franklin advised Ms. Altschuler of the situation.

On 10 March, Mr. Franklin presented his four-page report. He pointed out that of the eighteen short-term language objectives introduced by his classroom teacher, Edward had mastered fifteen. Other reports indicated his communication skills were improving. Mr. and Mrs. Washington faithfully attended the parent sign-class at Kinzie, a service not available at Spalding. Kinzie play leaders signed at recess; child-welfare attendants also signed, and the gym teacher was learning sign language. Assemblies and schoolwide activities were integrated and interpreted.

In addition to best developing Edward's communication skills, Kinzie School could meet all of the recommendations of the staffing team.

Public Law 94-142 requires that Edward Washington be provided with an appropriate education in the least-restrictive environment. Kinzie School clearly constitutes the least-restrictive environment.

The staff at Kinzie School is willing, capable, and committed to their responsibility to reach out to Edward Washington in order to provide him the greatest opportunity for social, emotional, academic, and physical development.

The staffing team concurred with Mr. Franklin's report. Despite Ms. Blatt's and Ms. Woods's objections, they decided that Edward should remain with his classmates.

On 11 March, Ms. Woods came back to Kinzie. She was *appalled* at the stance Mr. Franklin had taken in this case. She emphasized the word *appalled* and seemed to delight in saying it with a special affect, the dialect of the informed, one foreign to those out in the field. Her every word following *appalled* seemed to be elevated by this accent of significance. In the first place, she said that Mr. Franklin had overstepped his responsibilities as principal and his role in the special education staffings. Second, he was exaggerating his ability to determine the essence of staffing recommendations and to decide special education placements. He would find that he had erred in his judgment in the case of Edward Washington.

A few weeks later Mr. and Mrs. Washington presented Mr. Franklin with a deep, rich, wood-grained plaque with gold embellishments. It was engraved:

We thank you for implementing your God-given talent. Words alone cannot express our immense appreciation. You are what a principal stands for and we pray that others who follow you will embrace your approach regarding humanity.

The Washington Family

CHAPTER 13

The girl was at the store.
The girl was lost.
She was crying and crying.
And the man said What is wrong with you.
The man said here is your mother.
She ran and ran to her mother.
They had a big hug.

Markeeta's Book

Markeeta was a beautiful and good baby from her first breath. There were no complications during her birth, and it wasn't until Markeeta was about eight months old that Donna began to sense something was not quite right. Her daughter was a little too quiet, too good. But when her pediatrician assured her nothing was wrong, Donna thought maybe she was just being a nervous mother.

Then one day she saw a public service announcement on television, and she noticed that the child they were describing was a lot like Markeeta. Suspecting a hearing loss, she immediately called the telephone number on the screen. She received an appointment for diagnosis six months from that date. When the tests were finally completed, Donna was told that Markeeta, now sixteen months old, had such a profound hearing loss that there was little point in even getting her hearing aids. She would never speak.

Donna was devastated. Yet, when she got home, she somehow pulled enough of herself together to call the Siegel Institute for some direction. Fortunately for Markeeta and herself, she reached Theresa Jabaly, an especially supportive and caring audiologist who through the years had spoken to many mothers like Donna. Immediately, and for the next two hours, Theresa provided Donna the information and the understanding she so desperately needed. She explained that there were no generalizations; every child was different. She offered hope.

Markeeta was soon fitted with two ear-level hearing aids (her loss in one ear was profound, in the other ear, severe), and she was enrolled with Donna in Siegel's Hearing Impaired–Medical Academic Parent Support (HI-Maps) parent-infant program. At the same time they registered for the Chicago Public School parent-infant program. Donna intended to give Markeeta every advantage she could. Together, they began to learn sign language, and Markeeta began to learn to speak. A whole new world was opening up to them.

Markeeta entered Kinzie's full-time nursery at the age of three. Donna had visited various schools in the city and made this selection six months before her enrollment time. From Markeeta's first day, she was one of those special, radiant students that teachers appreciate. She was lovable and kind, generous and caring toward her playmates. She surrendered the buggy to the tiny girl with pleading eyes, shared a cookie with the dirty boy who perhaps had none at home, gave the blue crayon to the child who was grabbing for it, even though he had a horse in front of him to color.

Donna complied with all of the school directives. When Markeeta brought home her language notebook from the nursery, Donna was faithful in communicating with her about the "news," what happened in school that day. She took Markeeta on her lap, close enough to feel cuddled, but not so close that she couldn't see her mother's lips moving and watch her signs. They read over the "Today we made a turkey." They talked about the turkey's color, size, shape, and even its personality.

Each night Donna drew an awkward picture in the book illustrating what she and Markeeta had done at home. "Markeeta and Mommy went to the zoo. Markeeta saw the giraffes. They had long necks." And Donna signed and read her library books at bedtime. She continued taking sign language classes to improve her own skills, to be able to tell Markeeta everything. Markeeta's language began to surpass that of her classmates. She had more experiences; they were all communicated to her. Other children came back to school daily with "We watched TV," or no picture at all in their language books. Many returned without their books. Markeeta's language book was filled with news about making spaghetti, going to the park, buying mittens, and riding on the train.

Donna found out about a speech therapist who was willing to work with Markeeta for free if she could get her to the office. It meant a long train ride back and forth from the south side of the city to northern Evanston, but she pursued it. Markeeta's speech began to blossom, her "mommy" was perfectly clear.

When Markeeta was five, representatives from the March of Dimes Foundation visited Kinzie's deaf preschool classes. They recognized Markeeta's sparkling qualities. Like jiggled root beer, the effervescence bubbled from the tip of her curious chin to her smiling mouth, onto her shining innocent cheeks, up into her wondering, dark eyes, and finally settled in the hundreds of curly ringlets that framed her face. The visitors interviewed Donna and her daughter. Then Markeeta was enthusiastically named the Greater Chicago Area March of Dimes Poster Child.

During her interview Donna had explained that she wanted Markeeta to feel that she could do most anything she wanted. She didn't want her daughter to think her hearing loss had to stand in the way. And she didn't want her to hide her deafness or be ashamed of it. "I want her to talk and sign regardless of how other kids might react," Donna said. "When Markeeta has her picture taken, people sometimes ask me to take her hearing aids off. All I tell them is 'That is Markeeta, and if you take away her hearing aids, you're taking a part of Markeeta away too.' There are times," Donna admitted, "when I cry; especially when I see hearing kids do things that Markeeta will never be able to do, like enjoying music."

Three years after that interview, Donna cried happy tears when Markeeta amazed her by becoming the first deaf student accepted into the Kinzie School Band. She played the flute, and she enjoyed her very own music.

In 1987 while Edward was struggling for the least-restrictive environment of a self-contained classroom, Markeeta, along with Kristin, Sergio, and Jennifer, began spending part of the day learning in the regular classrooms. Markeeta and Kristin went to the first grade, and Jennifer and Sergio went to second grade for reading. Primary reading periods were scheduled so that Ms. Brownell could interpret in both classrooms. The board had no interpreters available for Kinzie. Ms. Brownell, in addition, advised the special ed homeroom teachers about which missing phonetic skills, such as rhyming sounds or correct word endings, needed to be retaught. Glor, Markeeta's and Kristin's special ed teacher, incorporated the phonics exercises in her speech lessons and allotted time for correcting the articulation of reading vocabulary words. Because of this little bit of extra tutoring, the girls were able to keep up in their very sophisticated "first reading group."

Deaf children not mainstreamed were using *Reading Milestones,* a series developed by Stephen Quigley at the University of Illinois especially for deaf students. It controlled vocabulary, syntax, and idiomatic expressions up to a point where the children could bridge to standard basal readers. In the past, none of Kinzie's deaf students had succeeded in bridging by age eleven, when they transferred to another deaf center; none had surpassed a standardized-reading-test score of third-grade level. These four mainstreamed students plunged right into the sink-or-swim basal readers. It was a challenge because of the broad vocabulary and the accelerated pace.

But Markeeta had her mom to help. Donna had become a Kinzie child-welfare attendant, a career service person hired to aid disabled children on the bus or in the classroom, and she was able to learn firsthand how she could help Markeeta at home. Along with studying reading with the first graders, Markeeta accompanied them to gym and library and communication arts. Glor began taking her class to music with the first graders, too. Markeeta especially enjoyed the silly song about the spaniel named Dan Dan Daniel, who "the more he'd chew, the more he grew."

In second grade some of Markeeta's classmates tried out for band; her closest hearing friends tried out for flute. Markeeta asked for a chance. Although the staff and Donna were doubtful, especially about the flute, I remembered an article in *Volta* about deaf students who had succeeded in band. Ms. Patenkin, the music teacher, read the copy of the story Brownell placed in her mailbox; and she decided that if Markeeta could pass the tryouts, she would allow her to be a band member.

Markeeta failed the first tryout, but she didn't give up. In third grade she tried again and made it. Soon other deaf children, inspired by her, decided to try out, too. At the conclusion of just one year in band, Markeeta lost interest and quit. But during that time Sergio, Jennifer, Jessica, Cesar, and Leo—all special education students—had become totally committed to saxaphone, flute, clarinet, and drums. They rode the early band-bus with the regular students; and Veda Park, another child-welfare attendant and a Kinzie parent like Donna, interpreted in sign language for the band's morning practice sessions.

Markeeta became a groundbreaker in more than band. While she was a kindergartener, her opportunities for free speech therapy were discontinued. At her annual audiological evaluation at Siegel, Theresa Jabaly recommended that speech therapy be a related service for Markeeta, a part of her IEP, Individual Educational Program, at Kinzie. The Chicago Public Schools audiologist did not make this recommendation, but the board's speech therapist did.

It was a very strange situation, Mr. Franklin observed, that all of the deaf children received a speech evaluation, but not one was ever recommended to receive speech services. When he inquired about this practice, he was told it was not the job of the Deaf Program's speech pathologist to offer therapy. Her function was to test. The teachers of deaf classes provided speech services. Chicago's hard of hearing children received speech therapy, but deaf children did not.

However, Markeeta was beginning to get along like a hard of hearing child. She was making good enough progress to try mainstreaming part-time. Therefore, based on the recommendations made at her staffing, Mr. Franklin arranged for Markeeta to get forty minutes per week of therapy from Ms. Brown, the speech pathologist who serviced Kinzie's hearing students with speech deficiencies. Although it was the first time Ms. Brown worked with a deaf child, she felt Markeeta was doing well. The board speech pathologist who had recommended therapy for Markeeta, however, was unexpectedly transferred to the other side of the city.

Second Grade Peer Journal

Markeeta: Yes I am happy it almost spring. Was the Valentine party fun?

Mirjana: Yes, it was fun. Don't you get bored sometimes? When I get bored it's really all the time. Can you tell me something I can do when I get bored? Im glad it is almost spring. Are you? What is the best Christmas present you got? My best was my parakeet. Her name is Chrissy. She is white and black. She is four months old.

Markeeta: Yes sometime I get bored. When I am bored then I play with my Barbie doll. My best Christmas present was a walking doll. My birthday is on March 17, 1989. I will be 8 year old. When is you Birthday? Will you have a party?

Mirjana: My birthday is December 18. I don't know if I will have a party. I hope I can have a party. Can You? What is your faverite Subject: My favrite subject is Math. Did you pinpal write you a long letter? My pinpal didn't. What is you favorite color? My favorite color is blue. your birthday is coming soon. I am 8 year old.

Markeeta: My favorite color is Blue too. My favorite subject is Math. I don't know if I will have a birthday party.

While Markeeta was happily making friends in second grade, Ms. Blatt reconvened her 1987 multidisciplinary staffing. Ms. Brown composed an addendum that summarized the board's position and was attached to Markeeta's staffing forms. In effect, speech therapy for Markeeta was canceled.

Donna disagreed. She wanted Markeeta to continue receiving the speech therapy she needed. She had no choice but to file for a due-process hearing, even against her own employer. Despite the consequences for herself, she was going to try for every advantage for Markeeta. The due-process hearing was scheduled for 24 February 1989, at the central office on Pershing Road.

At that meeting, the board took the position that Markeeta's speech and language deficiencies should be addressed by a teacher of deaf children assigned to work either with the classroom teacher or on a resource basis for sixty minutes per week. Ms. Blatt brought up the old argument that Mr. Franklin had refused to utilize a teacher, Ms. Banks, to provide individualized speech lessons. It was an attempt to delegate responsibility for a related service to a teacher of deaf students. The board due-process coordinator dismissed the remark, stating that the organization of teaching staff within the building was not an issue. What was an issue was the Free Appropriate Public Education (FAPE). Markeeta's advocate countered that the issues were whether Markeeta should receive the services of a speech pathologist in addition to the services of a teacher of deaf students, whether she was benefiting from the speech therapy she was receiving, and whether she would be discriminated against if those services were denied to her. It was up to the hearing officer to decide. In March of 1989 he did decide—*for* Markeeta.

In April the board requested a Level 2 Review, the second stage in a due-process hearing. The board cited the United

States Supreme Court decision in *Board of Hendricks Hudson Central School District, et al.* v. *Rowley* (1982). The board stated that it remained the applicable guideline, illustrated by *Kirkham* v. *McKenzie* (1988):

> The U.S. Supreme Court has said that the educational access extended by the Education of the Handicapped Act need not be the *best* program available, but it must be meaningful. Provision of FAPE does not require the LEA [Local Education Association] to maximize the potential of each handicapped child commensurate with opportunity provided non-handicapped children. The Supreme Court held that a FAPE is satisfied when the state provided personalized instruction with sufficient support services to permit the handicapped child to benefit educationally from that instruction.

Attached to the board's request for the Level 2 Review was a copy of the "acquisition-of-speech letter" from Ms. Blatt, signed by Ms. Woods.

Donna fortified herself against the aggravation, the anxiety, and suspense of the months ahead. She thought about how much Markeeta had accomplished because she didn't accept the expectations laid before her on that frightening day, the day when she learned Markeeta had a hearing loss. Remembering gave Donna the strength to continue. The audiologist had said Markeeta would never speak. Now the board said she would always speak like a deaf child. Donna heard the reassuring words again, "There are no generalizations. Every child is different."

The Level 2 hearing officer concluded that although there

were similarities between Markeeta's case and the Rowley case, the Court had suggested that determining which services are sufficient to give a child a free appropriate public education has to be decided on a case-by-case basis. In Markeeta's case, a speech therapist was necessary.

Kinzie had created a new kind of deaf program for the Chicago public schools with new kinds of expectations for its deaf students. The board took the view that Markeeta's articulation problems were to be expected, that they were typical of deaf children. Markeeta was not deviating from the expected level of performance of a child in a special education program.

But Markeeta was also a participant in a regular program where the levels of expected performance are higher. If the objective of special education is to move children to the mainstream, then educators must question how they define *expected level of performance.*

There was no question in Donna's mind about continuing to fight for Markeeta's right to speech therapy. She gave Markeeta another one of their big hugs.

I like to go to reading because reading is a lot of fun to talk to hearing children who know how to sign a little. I learned a lot from reading.

Kristin and I really love it because we are in a group everyday in reading. Ms. Salus has millions of books we like.

Now a lot of kids are mainstreaming and they love it!

Markeeta, deaf and fifth grade

CHAPTER 14

One of the biggest problems in education is attitude, everybody's attitude, teachers', parents', and, of course, all of the children's. Let's not forget the Board of Education and the government.

Nicky, 7th grade

Most of Kinzie had a positive attitude. A few of the regular teachers still talked of the old glory days, but current students were achieving. Kinzie kids always took high honors at the Math Counts Competition and in the Math Meet of the Academic Olympics. They were winners at the District Young Authors Conference, and two students were recognized at the citywide level. Two Kinzie students were among 105 chosen from 5000 nationwide for Young Writers Recognition. Kinzie had works of art and performances at Arts Festivals around the city. The reputation of the Kinzie Band was growing and they were invited to give concerts at special events. Attendance increased; suspensions decreased.

Some of the special ed teachers felt nostalgic about the traditional deaf program. It was more tranquil back then. But there were deaf children achieving, too. They were side-by-side with the hearing in academic classes and activities. Deaf children had entries in the Young Authors competition and Young Writers for the first time.

The entire school selected a cougar for its mascot and boasted of Kinzie's "Top Cats." The Cub Scouts had a pinewood derby. There was school beautification, career day, and the rejuvenated science fair, which involved special ed and regular kids in meaningful science-learning experiences. Arts activities continued, and Mr. Franklin was recognized for them by the Illinois Alliance for Arts Education. The Parents Club held its meetings on Wednesdays (parent sign-class day) so that more mothers of deaf students would attend.

Chicago-area teachers organized the state conference of the Illinois Teachers of the Hearing Impaired. Bell and Holy Trinity Schools assisted, but it was truly a Kinzie effort. I was president-elect, conference chair, Brownell, local area chairperson. Marcia did all of the artwork; Stan organized audiovisual equipment; Marilyn, David, and Flo handled registration. Everybody, including regular teachers, helped before and after school, assembling program books. Mr. Franklin led a state principals' meeting, and Glor and Julie were presenters. Daniel Ling and Stephen Quigley were the keynote speakers, and approximately five hundred professionals attended. Team effort made it run smoothly and proved Chicago Public School personnel were Top Cats too.

The four deaf students mainstreamed for academics had done well. They even made the honor roll. More students were recommended for mainstreaming. More parents were considering instituting due-process hearings to get speech services. But the triumphs were becoming tarnished by the turmoil that began to permeate the school.

Teachers of deaf classes felt that the due processes filed against the board were embroiling them in a civil war. They had been the traditional teachers of speech. Their students had never received speech therapy. They wanted what was best for their children, but the law said their children were entitled to the *appropriate* not the *best* programs. Were teachers appropriate and speech therapists best? Teachers didn't have all the battle facts; only the generals did. They began taking sides based on old alliances. Old wounds reopened, new ones appeared at tender areas. Directives from the board were interpreted as personal vendettas; some were. Strategies seemed to be in constant flux. Policies on speech changed every time the wind shifted. Suddenly, speech evaluations were no longer a regular part of the multidisciplinary staffing conference (MDC). Now the Deaf Program speech pathologist wasn't going to test their children either. The board was moving to a new consultative model under the direction of the coordinator for speech services.

The acquisition-of-speech letter reared its ugly head once more, and a special attachment came to me. I was to make a listing of the specific times I saw students in the deaf program individually for speech. Mr. Franklin directed me to ignore the forms. Duplicates and triplicates arrived. Ms. Altschuler suggested that they be complied with and the matter settled. Mr. Franklin reminded her that she settled it previously at the summer summit three years ago with Ms. Woods. Ms. Altschuler had no patience for it. She said to send the papers off. Classroom teachers were told to list their students' times for individual speech, and I transferred the records to the troublesome forms. Now, everyone was bothered by them.

One weekend a surprise fire destroyed Marcia's room. No one knew the cause, but the art room was totally gutted. Not one crayon was left unmelted. As if the emotional sparks weren't enough, Kinzie now had a genuine black pall of soot everywhere. The thick gray smoke had swirled through the vents and left a menacing layer of blackness over walls, drapes, carpeting, and the contents of each classroom. The entire deaf wing was darkened. It was a new challenge for Mr. Franklin to get the board workmen out to clean. Teachers were doubled up again, meeting temporarily in supply rooms, holding classes in any vacant area where they could carve a clean niche. Hours were spent grudgingly scrubbing the sooty casing off personal possessions.

School had to go on as normally as possible. Mainstream programs were growing. In addition to the four students who were doing well, Glor sent Ronnie and Adrian to the first grade. The first-grade class was large. Ronnie had trouble paying attention in his class of seven; it wasn't likely he would improve in a group of thirty-seven. Ronnie dropped his book and paper constantly during his group reading-time. He put his feet inside his desk during the seatwork period. Somehow, however, he kept up with his work for a while.

Adrian was three years older than the other children. Some of the first graders found him intimidating because he towered over them. Yet, he fell further and further behind academically because he never did his homework. Barbara Peters gave him special tutoring time each day, and still he was lagging. In the mornings Glor worked with only three children while her four other students were in reading. In the afternoon there wasn't enough time to fit in the group work and the individual help the four required to keep up in their regular classes.

More children were recommended by the school psychologist for mainstreaming; some were children who couldn't pay attention in their own special ed classes. Their teachers balked. The regular class enrollments were high. The regular teachers complained; they weren't included in the decision-making process. No interpreters were provided. Donna, although she was a child-welfare attendant, started interpreting; yet she felt that some of the children weren't behaving for her. David Trainor, the learning disabilities teacher, was asked to interpret two periods a day. It meant less time for learning disabilities remediation. The teachers were confused about making recommendations for mainstreaming or speech services. They wanted a policy. But the purpose of the IEP was to look at the children as individuals, not to slot them by policy. It was a hard time for Kinzie, a frustrating, tension-filled learning time.

The special education coordinators came out to the school for a staff meeting. Mr. Franklin smoked three cigarettes in succession outside the door of Ms. Brownell's room where the meeting was being held. Some teachers swore they saw smoke coming out of his ears as he introduced Ms. Blatt, Ms. Woods, and Dr. James Buchanan, coordinator of speech-and-language services. He said the coordinators wanted to clarify the board policy on speech services for deaf children.

Jane Blatt began. She said, "What teachers *believe* is necessary may or may *not* be necessary. The State Department of Education model says no speech therapy with deaf students. The board says teachers of deaf classes are the children's speech teachers." Stan asked why the board was stating this now; it wasn't new. The teachers had always taught speech.

Jane quoted *Ling*. *Ling* was the Bible Kinzie had adopted for its speech program. Jane said if the teachers didn't know how to teach speech, the board would arrange in-service meetings for them.

I found this comment insulting. I said that Kinzie had been providing its own speech in-services for years. Mr. Franklin clarified what Kinzie's speech program included, emphasizing that it was strongly organized.

Jane explained, "There are no speech therapists trained to work with deaf children available in Chicago. Children will not have an evaluation by a therapist unless some specific additional speech anomaly is noted. Teachers will provide speech evaluations of their own children."

Ms. Blatt continued, "We have to do the best we can. We are not a Cadillac system. What we have now is in jeopardy."

But she (in the spirit of goodwill) would not ask the audiologist to enumerate exactly how many of Kinzie's students had profound, severe, or moderate losses. A more scrupulous accounting might result in the closing of one or two positions at Kinzie, the loss of a few teachers. No one was sure of Kinzie's categorical totals, which students were the majority, but Jane's comments were menacing. We had slipped into a threatening "Twilight Zone" of wondering whose jobs were in the balance. Thank God the bell rang, and we could return to the relative sanity of our own rooms and our children.

Within a week Mr. Franklin received a letter from Fred Barnes. The director of Special Education had been informed that two Kinzie parents were filing due-process procedures in order to obtain the services of a speech pathologist. He wrote that he had previously stated his philosophy and mode of implementation for speech within the deaf program (the acquisition-of-speech letter). Mr. Barnes had been told that two Kinzie teachers were not performing classroom duties; and because Mr. Franklin was depriving deaf children of a speech program, either the two freed teachers were to begin tutoring in speech immediately or their positions were to be closed.

Mr. Franklin telephoned Mr. Barnes repeatedly. Finally, after a few days, Mr. Barnes returned his calls. Mr. Franklin attempted to explain that the request for due process had absolutely nothing to do with the provision of speech services by a teacher of deaf classes. Those parents perceived a meaningful distinction between speech provided by a teacher of deaf classes and speech provided by a certified speech-and-language pathologist.

Mr. Franklin corrected the statement that two teachers had been provided for speech and told Mr. Barnes that all Kinzie teachers were justified by the pupil-to-teacher ratio delineated by the state of Illinois. He declared that he deeply resented the erroneous statement that he was depriving deaf children of a speech program that was being implemented at other schools. He suggested that Mr. Barnes would be better served if he got his information from a more reliable source than Jane Blatt or Frances Woods.

When Mr. Franklin stated that Jane Blatt was the person with whom he consistently had problems, Mr. Barnes retorted, "I only have people work for me who care about children. Well," he concluded, "I want to clean up the situation at Kinzie. Tell Alice to have the coffee ready. I'll be out. We'll talk about it. You and Alice will just have to learn to get along with Jane and Frances."

Mr. Barnes came out a week later and visited Kinzie's classes for less than ten minutes. There wasn't enough time for coffee. Ten days afterward, he telephoned. "Mr. Franklin, I'll be honest. I saw some good things in your program but not enough speech and speechreading. And I understand that you have three team leaders floating around your building. I am not in favor of people running around. I want more people in direct contact with children."

Mr. Franklin reiterated that Kinzie had only one team leader, Ms. Brownell, and she spent a lot of her time interpreting. He had requested interpreters from the board and not received any.

Mr. Barnes asked, "Why? I can't understand why you're requesting interpreters for your mainstreaming program. If the children are mainstreamed, then they don't need interpreters." He continued, "Some of the people here in the central office have asked me to straighten Kinzie out so I've decided to send an investigative team to your school for two weeks, beginning this coming Monday. They will assess your program and offer recommendations. I've decided to put Jane Blatt in charge of this investigation."

Mr. Franklin could hardly restrain himself. This situation was so absurd it was surreal. In a just-barely-controlled voice, Mr. Franklin affirmed that he was proud of Kinzie's program and positive that any objective assessment of it would validate his own appraisal. However, he couldn't help but make the observation that it was ludicrous to appoint Ms. Blatt to evaluate Kinzie's program since she had been the source of the school's problems all along. The crux of the matter was that Ms. Blatt wanted to run the deaf program, to be the principal in absentia. This had been openly discussed at the summer meeting with Ms. Woods and Ms. Altschuler.

Mr. Barnes said he would make a concession. Ms. Blatt would only write the final report. Ms. Woods and Ms. Johnson, another deaf coordinator, would do the observations and the interviews instead of Jane. There would also be a school board member and a deputy superintendent out to visit on Monday.

Mr. Franklin met with the teachers and recounted his conversation with Fred Barnes. He explained that they would have visitors for the next two weeks. He said, "I don't feel as though I have to say anything further about this hypocritical assessment except that I would like you to carry on as you always do. I have always felt perfectly confident about people observing Kinzie's program. I have never been embarrassed by your conduct in the classrooms. I have always been proud to see you involved with your children in meaningful educational activities whenever I stop in."

On Monday a board member and an associate superintendent moved in and out of the deaf classrooms for about an hour. Ms. Johnson set up a schedule to spend some time in every classroom within the next two weeks. Ms. Woods didn't appear on Monday or Tuesday, but on Wednesday she arrived. She began her interviews by saying she was acting as part of a team assessing Chicago's total deaf program. She was sincerely interested in any Kinzie staff recommendations for future program development. "No, none of the other centers are receiving visitors." She talked to Mr. Franklin, Brownell, Marcia, and me.

Marcia had been added to her list because, according to the last acquisition-of-speech letter, she was a floater who should be tutoring in speech. Marcia, in reality, had moved from a deaf classroom to a full-time program in which she saw classes of deaf children for art activities all day and team-taught in most of the communication arts classes. Ms. Woods was interested in which art curriculum she was using and how she integrated her activities into the deaf program. Ms. Woods was, in addition, looking for specific ideas for art projects, simple crafts to do on a Saturday afternoon with her grandchildren. Marcia gave her a box of fabric crayons and showed her how the students had used them for T-shirts, flags, and quilts.

Ms. Brownell made an audiotape of her interview with Ms. Woods. She wanted any quotes attributed to her in Ms. Blatt's report verifiable. Ms. Woods told her the purpose of the study was to monitor the compliance of Kinzie's program. Brownell easily explained Kinzie's philosophy, curriculum, and materials; they were the meat of her job. She added that she now also did the testing and offered various kinds of support services to the teachers, including arranging in-service programs. She had to interpret for the mainstreamed students because the board had no interpreters for them. She also mentioned the short supply of psychologists and speech pathologists. It was a brief and professional exchange.

My interview moved from speech to communication arts to attendance at in-service and professional development meetings. Ms. Woods talked about working on her doctorate.

Mr. Franklin never bothered to discuss his interview, communicating its triviality by his lack of comment.

The sham evaluation united the deaf teachers, reviving "our side's" strong feelings of kinship. Their past pride in their group accomplishments was reborn. Teachers were not intimidated by the central office personnel, but they were annoyed by this waste of their energy, which was being diverted from their students.

Ms. Johnson met with Mr. Franklin at the conclusion of her two weeks of visiting classes. She said, "My general observation is that Kinzie has a well-run deaf program. The teachers are warm and receptive and open. As a rule of thumb, we might expect that 10 to 15 percent of the students might require the services of a speech pathologist. I agree that speech from a teacher of deaf classes does not belong on an IEP as a related service. And for your information, Frances said to me, 'Maybe it *is* the coordinator who is creating the problems at Kinzie.'"

Three days after the visits were completed, Fred Barnes retired. No report ever surfaced.

CHAPTER 15

I love Mommy.
Mommy and Daddy "talk, talk, talk."
I get headache. Leslie sleep.
I watch T.V.
Mommy is good to me.

Joey

In his letter to Mr. Franklin, Fred Barnes had mentioned two students involved in due-process procedures for speech. They were Markeeta and Joey. Joey's parents had begun the due-process procedure in the midst of Kinzie's turmoil, before Markeeta's case was decided. Joey was main-streamed successfully into the regular kindergarten part-time, but Joey was very different from Markeeta.

Joey's life began in crisis. He was born two months pre-maturely and weighed only four pounds, four ounces. On the third day of his life, he developed respiratory problems and was hurried to Loyola's Neonatal ICU. He was severely hypo-tonic and did not suck. Joey suffered three seizures during his first month. But finally, after thirty days, he stabilized, gained enough strength to nurse, and was allowed to leave the hospital with his parents.

Joey seemed to reach developmental milestones a little later than most children; however, when one considered his (gestational age) instead of his chronological age, Joey seemed to be holding his own. He held his head up at 3 months (1 month), crawled on his belly at 9 months (7 months), sat unsupported and pulled to a stand at 11 months (9 months), and walked independently at 16 months (14 months). Joey's mother, Shelly, brought him to occupational-therapy sessions faithfully, beginning when he was only one month old, so that he would acquire the motor skills he was slow in developing.

Joey's speech and language were severely delayed. He vocalized, "ah-ah-ah" for whatever he wanted. His first true words, "thank you," weren't spoken until he was almost four years of age. At three Joey had an adenoidectomy and placement of pressure-equalizing tubes (bilaterally) because of ear infections and excessive fluid accumulation in the middle ear. After a Chicago Public School case study at this same time, Joey was enrolled in speech therapy at Hale School.

One day, a relative noticed that Joey didn't respond to excessively loud rock music. Audiological testing revealed a severe-to-profound bilateral sensorineural hearing loss. Joey was fitted with a hearing aid within the month and staffed into Kinzie's deaf preschool program. He was three and one-half years old. The board arranged for occupational therapy, but his speech services were discontinued.

Shelly had Joey's speech and language evaluated at Saint Xavier College Ludden Speech and Language Clinic on September 20, 1988. Joey was almost seven. As part of an expressive language test, he was shown a photograph of a dog lying under a chair; and he responded, "dog, chair, under, chair, dog." A girl standing behind a chair prompted, "girl under chair." At the sight of two girls coloring, Joey said, "girl, girl color picture." For a photo of two girls sitting beside one another, one of whom was eating a sandwich, he offered, "girl sandwich, girl no sandwich." And finally, for books Joey became very animated, "book, read, I have those; climbing the beanstalk."

The speech pathologist at Ludden felt that Joey's speech prognosis was excellent because he was so eager to achieve.

He participated enthusiastically in the speech games, and he showed improvement immediately. He had no additional oral-motor problems; he imitated language well. Joey was very bright, and his parents were eager to help him in any way that they could.

Millions and Millions of Moons
Moons is dark. Millions and millions and millions moons. The moons is many world. Make dark moons. But is Halloenn moon. Make rain moon. But is too many moons. Is finshed moon.
Now we have sun. Sun is day swimming. Long is sun warm day. Is summertime and warm.
Is moon come.

Joseph

The Ludden pathologist recommended that speech therapy be a part of Joey's IEP at Kinzie. In her report she stated that Joey had always needed speech services. It was documented in his first case study at age three. It was recognized in all of his subsequent IEPs. P.L. 94–142 gave him the right to receive the speech services he needed.

"In closing, consider the following: Joe is being taught in a specialized setting by a teacher who specializes in the education of hearing impaired children. It is imperative his speech/language needs be addressed by one who specializes in disorders of communication, i.e., a Speech-Language Pathologist. This is his privilege by law."

Joey was mainstreamed into kindergarten part-time, into gym, library, music, and communication arts. His teacher, Flo, was charmed by his stories, which tumbled out abundantly in a jumble. Everything about Joey was a tumble and a jumble; he was all boy. Yet, Flo could see that with the proper assistance Joey was going to put his school experience all together and make sense of it. He was intelligent enough to do it, and Shelly would help.

Joey's parents requested an impartial due-process hearing in November of 1988. In December the Illinois State Board of Education appointed a mediator. Illinois' mediation service is designed as an alternative to the due-process hearing, a means of resolving disagreements regarding the appropriateness of special education and related services of children enrolled in Illinois public schools. This service is administered and supervised by the Illinois State Board of Education and is provided at no cost to the parties.

In mediation, neither party is asked to abandon basic beliefs about the student's ability; rather, the parties are asked to consider alternatives that could be incorporated into the student's program, to be realistic about both the student's capabilities and the local district's obligations and resources.

For Joey the mediation process resulted in recommendations for more evaluations. Joey participated in another speech and another psychological testing session. There would be another meeting to consider the results of these latest tests.

A multidisciplinary staffing conference (MDC) took place at Kinzie on 15 February 1989. Ms. Dawber provided Joey's most recent independent evaluations and once again requested speech therapy. The board refused to provide the service. Shelly wrote a letter of rejection restating her request for a speech pathologist to provide services to Joey. Mr. Franklin, Flo, Pat Bradshaw, the school psychologist, and I each wrote paragraphs of disagreement with the board's plan for Joey's instructional program. Mr. Franklin stated that there was no "extended teacher of speech," none had ever been provided to Kinzie School. Pat wrote that her concerns were related to the "psychoeducational and social/emotional adjustment Joey must make in the mainstreamed environment where his speech production is radically different from [that of] his mainstreamed peers." Flo and I stated our feelings that Joey's speech could improve with individual tutoring.

A hearing officer was selected, and the due-process hearing was scheduled for 23 February, at Kinzie. The hearing was rescheduled for 6 April and then for 20 April. Preparations had been ongoing for months. Twenty witnesses were called to testify, including eight Kinzie staff members. Shelly was represented by the Northwestern University School of Law Legal Clinic, with Laura Miller acting as supervising attorney, and three student attorneys. The small, stuffy assistant principal's office where the proceedings took place was packed with too many tense bodies. Cramped around a long table like guests at the Mad Hatter's Tea Party, they kept exchanging their conflicting opinions hour into hour, day into day, kept closing the teapot lid on the tiny dormouse who, again and again, persistently popped up his head for breath.

But this was not a Lewis Carroll fantasy for Shelly. It was Joey's real-life biography that was being written here. And some of the ghost writers brought at best an impersonal, cursory encounter with her son as their expertise. It was too much to bear for a mother, to suffer through these smug declarations.

Mr. Franklin read the frustration on Shelly's face. That frustration colored the timbre of his voice as he began his statement:

The position of the central office staff seems to be that Joseph Dawber is not eligible for speech services from a speech-language pathologist because he is deaf. Children in the regular classroom are eligible, children in other special ed programs are eligible, children in hard of hearing programs are eligible.

The board says that deaf children's needs for speech and language are met by the deaf program, by the certified teacher of the deaf. All the camouflage thrown over this program, with lectures about speech and language from his own teacher, and additional speech and language from a second teacher of the deaf with exactly the same qualifications and certification as his classroom teacher, can't negate the fact that a speech pathologist is vastly more qualified in the area of speech.

Secondly, the board says Joey is accessing his instructional program. This is a criterion that is imposed on no other children in determining their eligibility. That, in itself, should invalidate this rationale.

But if we look carefully at the board's position; what are they really saying? They are saying that because this boy is making good, even remarkably successful progress in the deaf program, he doesn't need speech service.

But what is good progress in a deaf program? It is progress in a program that has been a dismal failure in what should be the primary objective of every program— to move children into the mainstream of life, in this instance, to move children from the deaf to the hearing world. This is not intended to be a criticism of our program or our teachers. I believe in them. It is the nature of the disability in many instances that precludes the true transition from the deaf to the hearing world. The board is saying though that "deaf is deaf"—be satisfied with progress in that program.

Now we have a child who is perceived by some experts to be able to make the transition if he is provided with speech-and-language therapy. We shouldn't be bickering and debating about this service. We should all be celebrating the success he's had so far, celebrating the fact that his hearing aids make such a dramatic difference for him, celebrating his intelligence, and celebrating the love and perseverance of his mother, who hasn't allowed herself to be beaten down by the system, who has willingly subjected herself to the draining process of going through interminable staffings, testing sessions. . . .

I have watched Ms. Dawber throughout the course of this hearing. I've seen her face light up when Joey's teachers and others who know him have described his successes, and I've seen the look of anguish and disbelief on her face when people who wouldn't know Joey Dawber if he walked through this door talk about what he can and can't do. This is not a wild-eyed, fanatic parent who is asking for something unreasonable or inappropriate. This is an intelligent, concerned, loving mother who simply wants to give her child the opportunity he deserves to be able to function in a hearing world.

The testimony and the interrogation lasted for two days, but in May the Level 1 Hearing Officer decided that Joey was entitled to speech therapy.

On 8 June the board requested an appeal of the decision. The board pursued its argument that the Education for the Handicapped Act (EHA) and the Illinois Administrative Code defined "related services" as those required to assist a child benefit from *special education*. Since Joey Dawber was on the honor roll, he didn't need speech therapy.

In July, attorney Laura Miller asked for a dismissal of the board's appeal on the grounds that it was not moving in a timely fashion. Anticipating dismissal, the board withdrew its appeal in August. The Level 1 decision was binding.

With Joey's case resolved, Laura Miller turned to the rights of other deaf children in Chicago who were being refused needed speech services. She filed a complaint with the U.S. Department of Education, Office for Civil Rights (OCR) against the Chicago Board of Education for violation of Section 504 of the Rehabilitation Act on the ground that the board was engaging in a systemic denial of the related service of individual speech therapy to deaf children.

Ms. Miller reported that not one child in the deaf program at Kinzie School was provided with speech therapy from the board. The board offered various and contradictory reasons for this, all of which were in violation of federal and state law, including: (1) so long as deaf children are progressing in school without speech therapy they are not entitled to that service; (2) individual speech therapy is too restrictive since it is offered outside of the classroom and without other children; (3) where the cause of the speech problem is deafness, there is no entitlement to the related service of speech therapy; and (4) teachers of the deaf provide services that are comparable in type and quality to those offered by speech pathologists. She stated that the "too restrictive" rationale was a perverse distortion of the "least-restrictive environment." Related pull-out services are designed to facilitate mainstreaming. To deny children related pull-out services because the pull-out time itself is restrictive is to deny them the opportunity to function in a less-restrictive classroom environment. Deaf children who do not have facility in speech run a much greater risk of failing in the mainstream setting. Ms. Miller concluded, "Nothing in *Rowley* supports the proposition that if a child is able to learn to read, write, and do math problems, he has no entitlement to learn to speak."

OCR initiated an investigation. In 105 days their office would issue a letter of findings. If a violation had occurred, the board had 195 days to move into compliance; otherwise, OCR enforcement action could result in an administrative hearing to determine whether Federal funds should be terminated.

Within ten days the board was to send OCR a computer printout of all the deaf students in the Chicago public schools, including the dates of their last speech-and-language evaluations and a report of whether they were receiving service from a speech pathologist. The names of all speech-and-language pathologists assigned to public schools serving deaf children, the names of all district coordinators and itinerant instructional teachers (IITs) serving the deaf, and any written policy statement, description of district practice, and narrative of the district's position regarding the circumstances under which speech-and-language services were provided to deaf children (the acquisition-of-speech letter) were also requested. A warning was included: "Please be advised that individuals filing a complaint or participating in an investigation of a complaint are protected by Departmental regulations which prohibit harassment or intimidation."

OCR interviewed speech pathologists, teachers, program coordinators, and a principal who served deaf students in the district during the 1988–89 school year. The speech pathologists stated that they were aware of and followed an unwritten policy that deaf students could not benefit from speech-and-language services and that if this service were needed, teachers of deaf students were required to provide the service.

Consequently, speech pathologists rarely recommended that speech therapy be provided to deaf students. Teachers of deaf children as well as program coordinators also were aware of this unwritten policy and felt obligated to make recommendations consistent with it.

The district identified 376 students as being hard of hearing or deaf. OCR randomly selected and reviewed the educational files of eighty (21 percent) of these students to determine whether appropriate evaluation and placement procedures were followed with respect to the provision of speech-and-language services. Bell, Skinner, Kinzie, and M. Jackson, four schools having the largest enrollments of deaf students, were selected for review. All of the students in the sample were identified as having either severe or profound hearing disabilities. Of the eighty files reviewed only one student had an IEP indicating the need for speech therapy as a related service.

OCR found that all of the deaf students received a speech-and-language case study evaluation. Although a group of persons knowledgeable about each student met and discussed the speech-and-language evaluation results during multi-disciplinary staff conferences, only one of the educational programs included speech-and-language services. Except for three students at Kinzie, no student files contained documentation that conference participants even considered whether the students required speech/language services. At Kinzie, three files documented a determination that students *did not need* speech-and-language services. Finally, in one Kinzie file it was noted that in 1986 the parents of a student requested speech therapy; however, there was no indication that this request was acted upon.

District staff confirmed that none of the students attending M. Jackson, Skinner, and Kinzie whose files were reviewed by

OCR received speech-and-language services during the 1988–89 school year. On the basis of evidence submitted by both the complainant and the district and of testimony provided by relevant witnesses, OCR determined that the district categorically denied speech-and-language services to deaf students.

On 10 November 1989, the board entered into an agreement to remedy the situation. As of the beginning of the 1989–90 school year, the unwritten policy denying speech-and-language therapy for deaf or hard of hearing students was rescinded. Deaf students would be evaluated and considered for speech-and-language services and would receive these services based on procedures consistent with Section 504.

No one monitored this settlement. The Office of Civil Rights did not have staff available. The agreement was a paper tiger, for the bureaucracy never budged. In June of 1990, Laura Miller filed a class-action suit, *Calvin G.* v. *The Board of Education of the City of Chicago and Ted D. Kimbrough*, superintendent of the Chicago Public Schools. In July of 1991 the board settled out of court, and Laura Miller and her staff resolved to monitor the system's compliance. The Tea Party was over. The Mad Hatter had shut his mouth and taken his seat; the dormouse was free to come out of his teapot, to speak, and then to explore the variety of delicacies spread across the table.

My secret place is beautiful. To get there, all you do is close your eyes and see the pretty flowers and fish swimming in the clear river. There are pretty animals too; you will love them. They are nice and friendly. There is beautiful grass, trees, the sky and soft lovely clouds.

This is only lonely if you're feeling lonely, unloved, angry or sad. This is only for children. It's like an angel's playground. When the rainbow appears, that means it's time to come back.

Saritha, third grade

Congratulations! You have been elected by your peers to represent them and their children at a most historic time in our city. As a member of your Local School Council, you will undertake one of the most difficult tasks facing our city and our nation, the fundamental re-evaluation and restructuring of our schools.

The eyes of the nation are on Chicago. We have done what most people think about and talk about, but only a few have the courage to do—get involved and rally together to help our children. Now the fate of our children depends upon you. You must continue to work together. You must open yourselves to new ideas and to new partnerships. You must continue to reflect your will and your courage in the decisions you make.

> Yours truly,
> Richard M. Daley, Mayor

School reform was now the law. Kinzie's principal, parents, and staff had been struggling together for the past seven years to meet students' needs. They had written letters and demonstrated at board meetings to get auditory-training units for the deaf children. They had worked with outside agencies to make ear molds. They had begged and borrowed to acquire band equipment. They had written grants and sold candy and popcorn to bring arts programs and assemblies to the children. They had won awards to obtain computers. They had persisted through due-process hearings to provide speech services. Together they had worked within the system, around the system, and even against the system when they were forced to do so. And together, they had succeeded in making Kinzie a better place to learn.

Secretary of Education William Bennet breezed through the windy city and left Chicago's public schools with the moniker "Worst in the Nation." An investigative series in the *Chicago Tribune* depicted in graphic detail some of the most depressing scenarios in public school classrooms, halls, playgrounds, and neighborhoods. Citywide morale was rock bottom, buried by the rubble of recurring teacher strikes, entombed by the landslide of seemingly insurmountable urban problems.

Parents, community groups, business leaders, and professional school reformers, frustrated with the board of education and the superintendent, were convinced that their demands for improvement would forever be ignored. Under the leadership of Mayor Harold Washington, they formed an education coalition. The 1987 teacher strike, which lasted for nineteen days, had been their "last straw." This new and resolute education alliance lobbied state legislators for school-based management.

School-based management was education's version of changes that were made in the surrounding business community. In 1900 the Chicago area had encompassed fifty-one independent school districts. By the middle of the century there was only one, consolidated and centralized, serving more than a half million students. During that same period major businesses, aiming to increase efficiency and eliminate waste, had also become centralized; however, as they expanded even further, businesses found that their size was increasingly inhibiting their efficiency. No longer able to manage their transactions satisfactorily from a central location, they opened branch offices and allowed decisions to be made at the local level. By the 1970s and 1980s businesses had decided on decentralization as the best method for increasing productivity.

Likewise, in the 1970s and 1980s, national studies attacked the burgeoning nonproductiveness of large urban school districts. In Chicago statistics revealed that 43 percent of public school students dropped out before graduation, and 67 percent read below the national average. The education coalition challenged Chicago schools to follow the lead of the business community, to increase the productivity of their students by decentralizing.

Educational research by Goodlad, Brown, and a growing number of professionals supported decentralization. Educators began to argue that decisions made at the local level were better. Decision makers within the schools assumed ownership for their initiatives and became committed to accomplishing their goals. Decision makers within the schools knew what their students lacked, and consequently, what they needed. And decision makers within the schools were more willing to change. Historically, changes ordered by central office mandates were most often resisted.

In 1988 Public Law 85–1418, the Chicago School Reform Act, created 542 school boards for the city. The law gave these 542 Local School Councils a fistful of absolute powers. First, they were to select their principal, negotiate his contract, and evaluate his performance. Administrative tenure was abolished. Second, they were to develop a three-year school improvement plan, and third, draw up a lump-sum budget. Fourth, they were responsible for advising the principal concerning attendance, disciplinary policies, and the allocation of teaching resources and staff. Last, they were to receive training.

At Kinzie a strong educational community had evolved

from past struggles, a homeostatic entity within which principal, teachers, and parents shared duties. Now, it appeared that the legislators were tampering with this equilibrium, clearly shifting power to the parents and community. There would be six parents, two community members, and only two teachers along with the principal on the council. The participants with the most school experience and expertise were going to be in the minority.

Kinzie Parents Club members moved into active roles in the Local School Improvement Council (LSIC), the precursor of the Local School Councils to be elected in October 1989. There was a smooth transition. Gradually, however, the tenor of the LSIC meetings became strained. One parent began to interpret her role too seriously for the other members. Ms. Szypanski became overly conscientious about her new responsibilities and the expectations the law offered her. She was in the school every day checking on the toilet tissue in the bathrooms, the light bulbs in the halls, and the movements of the janitorial personnel. At first a noticeable improvement occurred and the custodial staff became more conscientious, but the limit was soon reached, and the nit-picking began. Tempers flared; a wall of resistance rose, buttressed by the building engineer.

Ms. Szypanski was forced to turn her attention to curricular matters instead. She became concerned that the second-grade teacher wasn't doing enough spelling. I hadn't included all of my communication arts students in the last assembly. The eighth-grade teacher needed direction with the science fair. The third-grade teacher devoted too much time to handwriting. All of these shortcomings and many more needed to be addressed in the school improvement plan.

But the other LSIC parents weren't as scrupulous about determining the local school improvement plan as their president, and they didn't have as much time to spend in the school building. Ms. Szypanski reprimanded them for what she perceived to be their shortcomings, their lack of concern and commitment. Her aggressive badgering, which included an actual nudge and a shove on occasion, drove some of the parents off the council. Ms. Ellsworth, secretary of the LSIC, resigned.

> I feel in the past we had very good intentions, as well as positive things happening for the improvement of the school. I do, however, feel this council now is not being handled for the best interest of the children, staff, and general well being of the school. I do not agree with this position, and I do not feel as though I want to remain part of this council.

But Ms. Szypanski only increased her resolve to re-create the instructional programs at Kinzie. She wrote her own personal educational plans that listed specific levels of achievement for students, particular classroom activities to be implemented, and directives for teachers. She stuffed them in faculty mailboxes. To this correspondence, she attached a list of parents who supposedly endorsed her plan.

Parents were furious when they learned that their meeting attendance sheet had been misrepresented as a statement of support for Ms. Szypanski's initiative. Angrily, they disavowed any connection with Ms. Szypanski's instructional plan. Most of these parents had been actively involved in developing the existing Kinzie programs, and they were pleased with the progress. Individually, they sent letters of apology to the staff expressing their feelings of frustration. They were fed up with the adversarial tone of Ms. Szypanski's meetings and with her singular, antagonistic drive to manage school affairs.

Dear Kinzie Faculty,

I was informed upon arriving at school that a meeting we held in the summer of the Local School Improvement Council was being discussed. At that meeting we were told to read over some proposals. It was suggested that on the first day of school this plan should be given out to Mr. Franklin and the staff of Kinzie School. We stated that we did not agree with these proposals. We are just parents who are interested in the well-being of our children. I am very upset that this plan went out to you. What we all signed was the fact that we had attended the meeting, not that we agreed with this plan.

Ms. Alvarez

Ms. Szypanski persisted, submitting to Mr. Franklin almost daily at first requests, then demands, and finally remonstrances on a variety of topics. He began a log because if his responses weren't delivered to her expeditiously, Ms. Szypanski cleverly maneuvered through the Pershing Road administration until she found some board bureaucrat who would give her a confirmation of her wishes. It was convenient that the district superintendent was housed in the same building as Kinzie. Every school grievance could be registered with Ms. Altschuler as well as with Mr. Franklin. And complaints against the district could be reported easily as well. Ms. Altschuler wasn't using the district rooms to the satisfaction of the Kinzie LSIC. The district wasn't responding quickly enough to LSIC concerns.

Ms. Szypanski also filed complaints in the alderman's office on nearby Archer Avenue. His office staff telephoned the school and the district office regularly regarding her harassment. She repeatedly made it known to all that it was her *council* that soon would have the power to decide just who the principal would be and also who would become the next district superintendent.

Ms. Altschuler was extremely annoyed by Ms. Szypanski. She was angry with Mr. Franklin for not controlling this nuisance. The woman should have been dealt with at the school level, not been around to pester her. At the same time, Ms. Altschuler was fed up with the speech controversies born in his building, growing throughout the system, and coming of age in the courts. She felt that the speech question should have been settled at the conclusion of her summer summit years ago, but Mr. Franklin let it rise like the phoenix and singe them all. The fact that parents were filing due processes was a black mark against him. The controversy had gotten out of hand with her old friend Fred.

For all of these reasons, she was petulant when she met with Mr. Franklin in her office regarding his annual performance evaluation. Always following pedagogic protocol, however, she began on a positive note; she complimented his appearance as impeccable. She commented, too, that it was admirable the way he responded to his students. She observed him on the playground, in the lunchroom, and the halls. His fire drills were still imperfect; but, in general, he managed his school well. Attendance was good; there were very few serious discipline problems. His reports were punctual and exemplary. Yet, she was compelled to lower his rating. There was nothing he could say. There was just too much trouble associated with him. In seven years he had never learned the golden rule.

But Ms. Altschuler's criticisms were secondary now to the crisis festering in the Local School Council. It was imperative for Mr. Franklin and his staff to mobilize the parents who had been antagonized by Ms. Szypanski. They had to be persuaded to resume their participation in Kinzie's Local School Improvement Council, not to drop out, not to allow Ms. Szypanski to destroy what they had already accomplished. Teachers and parents together had to develop a slate of candidates who could work harmoniously for the benefit of all Kinzie's students. As a team they had to energetically campaign for their slate. They had to publicize to all Kinzie parents the character of the existing council and motivate enough of them to come out to the candidates' forum. Finally, they had to move the majority to vote for their endorsed slate. The politics of reform presented a new challenge to the Kinzie community just when they thought they had finally solved their biggest problems.

Ms. Szypanski promoted her own Local School Council candidates with her husband as front-runner. He opened his campaign with the ominous declaration: "I don't believe in the old axiom: If it ain't broke, don't fix it. I believe in the constant drive for improvement, and I am willing to devote the time to it."

Shelly Dawber agreed to run for a parent position. In a local newspaper interview Shelly explained how she had fought for more than a year to get a speech therapist for the deaf students at Kinzie. She won the battle and believed that the fight taught her some valuable lessons, lessons that would help her as a member of the council. Ms. Dawber didn't see a need for a lot of changes at Kinzie, but she did see a need for change in the administration of the Chicago schools. She called Joey's special education program excellent. "It is a very thorough program. Speech therapy is offered to all special education students who need it now, and the students are evaluated every three years. I am very happy with Joey's school, its principal, and its teachers."

Those parents who had formed the backbone of Kinzie's Parents Club took up the banner once again. The endorsed slate included Shelly, Peggy Ellsworth, Maria Alvarez, Carol Krachic, Marilyn Peters, Nancy Borsino, Delores Conners, Terry Atkins (Kinzie's annual Santa Claus) and teachers, Marilyn Steiner, who was the teachers' union representative, and myself. Ms. Szypanski campaigned zealously at the school door right up until the polls closed, and so did our parents. The final vote affirmed those candidates endorsed by the Parents Club. Parents and staff members who had been forced to expend an enormous amount of energy on political issues could now focus again on their primary concern, educating the children.

Because Kinzie had elected parents and teachers of children with disabilities to the council along with neighborhood parents and community members, communication between the groups increased, understanding deepened, and more support for mainstreaming throughout the school was elicited. Ms. Krachic, the first Local School Council chairperson, had been actively involved in the educational program from the time her twenty-four-year-old daughter was a kindergartner here. Presently, her son was benefiting from learning-disabilities services. She attended the Friends of Special Education meetings with Shelly, and together they planned presentations for all of Kinzie's parents.

More deaf children were included in library and music classes. Scheduling was arranged so that their teachers could attend with them and interpret or team teach whenever it was possible. A formal schoolwide deaf awareness program was initiated. Although some background information on hearing loss was a regular part of the sign-language classes and Communication Arts program, these lessons did not reach every student in the school. Some first graders still thought that you could become deaf by eating too many chili peppers.

Barbara Chirlos and Julie Gonwa, preschool teachers of deaf children, developed a traveling show that featured reassuring Dr. Gonwa and likable Little Barbara, who had a hearing loss. Each classroom teacher was enlisted to role-play Barbara's mother, who was learning about deafness, just like the kids. All together they discovered, with the help of Dr. Gonwa, that Little Barbara was deaf. They learned just what that meant for Barbara, what things she could still do the same as they did, and what things she had to do differently. They found out what might have caused Barbara's hearing loss: not hot peppers, but perhaps measles, other illnesses, or even medicines that were too strong. It could be that Barbara was born deaf because her mom, dad, or grandparents were deaf.

Hearing children got the opportunity to try on hearing aids. They experienced sounds made louder but not clearer. They found out that wearing a hearing aid was a little like listening to a radio not tuned in. Now they could understand why it was so difficult for deaf children to develop good speech.

The students also practiced communicating with Barbara using speechreading and trying sign language. They really sympathized with Kinzie's deaf kids when they discovered that in order to learn, they always had to watch and pay attention every minute they were in school. If the deaf children looked out the window at a squirrel on a nearby telephone pole, they might miss seeing the formula they needed to solve a problem or finding out the correct answer to an important question. How lucky they were themselves to be hearing and to be able to watch the snow drifting on the ledge and still hear the teacher talking.

CHAPTER 17

Once upon a time there was a class with millions of students. Some had to stand, some sat on chairs, and others had to sit on the floor. It took ten minutes to collect all of the students' papers. After one month there wasn't enough paper to pass out to the students, and the teachers had problems getting the students' names in their attendance books.

But everything worked out when they got a new teacher. Ms. Sandusky came.

Juan, sixth grade

The most significant result of the educational reform law was the distribution of real dollars to the local schools, coupled with the power of the Local School Council to determine just how to spend them. Prior to reform there were no discretionary funds available to principals. The new law released state Chapter 1 money.

In 1973 Illinois legislators had revised the state funding formula so that districts with low-income students would receive additional money. They designated it "Chapter 1 funding," a bonus to provide for the high cost of educating children from disadvantaged areas. Because suburban legislators insisted on limits, districts could count no more than 75 percent of their students as low-income even if the true figure was greater. Legislators later dropped the limit to 62 percent. Because 70 to 80 percent of Chicago's students come from low-income homes, city schools in poor neighborhoods were still shortchanged.

In addition, the Chicago Urban League discovered that instead of reserving its Chapter 1 money for disadvantaged schools, the board was spreading these funds throughout the system. When the league took legal action, a new law was passed requiring Chicago to earmark 60 percent of Chapter 1 funds for schools with low-income children. The board continued to use most of this money to pay for basic services such as kindergarten and school libraries. Approximately 20 percent was even spent on central office staff. Reform brought about a real revolution when it forced the board to distribute Chapter 1 funds to individual schools. Based on actual low-income enrollment numbers, the money would follow the child.

Local School Councils were allowed to budget Chapter 1 funds only on supplemental programs, not on basics. Six general categories were acceptable: early childhood instruction, reduced class size, student enrichment, attendance improvement, remedial education, and staff-and-curriculum development. At Kinzie the council decided to use this bonus money to buy a teacher. In order to decrease the overcrowding in the fourth-grade class, Ms. Sandusky was hired. During her interview, Mr. Franklin asked what had become a standard query to all Kinzie applicants. Ms. Sandusky answered that she was willing to accept children with disabilities in her regular class.

This was her first teaching assignment. Mary Kay Sandusky had eighteen students in the split fourth-grade class, and she had Markeeta and Kristin, who were now mainstreamed half of the day, with an interpreter. Mary Kay didn't know what to expect from the deaf children; and she was nervous about the interpreter, an adult on hand to witness the mistakes of a novice teacher. She felt she had to explain her every action: why she gave spelling tests on Thursday instead of

Friday, how she chose the vocabulary words for study, her criteria for picking students for errands. She offered an elaborate argument for educational games to justify the one period a week they played "On the Road to Zanzibar."

The interpreter listened. She didn't question. But she did offer little suggestions about seating, where Mary Kay stood when she lectured, how she used the chalkboard, the overhead projector, and the handouts. The interpreter, it turned out, was someone Mary Kay could talk to about changes in the class that would benefit her two deaf students. She was not a judgmental but a caring person. And Mary Kay discovered that in accommodating the deaf girls, she was helping all of her visual learners as well. She was even making things easier for herself. Writing a page number on the chalkboard instead of just saying it saved repeating it over and over again.

It was not long before Mary Kay decided that she wanted to communicate directly—personally with her two deaf students. Kinzie had a weekly sign class for staff; but as a beginning teacher, she just couldn't spare the time to attend. She was too busy in the morning, preparing her lessons. She registered herself and her mother in a community college class instead, and they practiced communicating at home each night. After only a few lessons, Mary Kay jumped right in and began signing to Markeeta and Kristin. They opened up like sunflowers in August. Her eighteen students followed her lead.

Mary Kay had been apprehensive, but she never showed it. In her deep-set eyes gleamed only her intensity, her determination to succeed. Hair bobbing, she bounced through the halls with strong, swift steps, leading her class decisively, propelled by her energy and enthusiasm. Her voice was loud enough to project over the exclamations of curious fourth graders sticking needles through balloons, spinning eggs, and racing soup cans. She was comfortable sitting on an empty desk right in their midst—at the same time with them and on top of them. They learned she was a teacher and a person. She told them she liked wind surfing and could play the organ. Like them, she had pets—a dog named Duke of Earl and two birds, Fritz and Blues. She had taught kindergarten students for a little while, but they knew she liked fourth graders best.

In her second year, Mary Kay team taught with Marilyn Steiner, a teacher of deaf students who brought along her entire class. There were thirty-two children, divided into two groups by math ability. Marilyn worked at the front board, Mary Kay at the back. It was helpful for her to see a special education teacher in action. They cooperated in creating the lessons. Both math groups were integrated; Mary Kay was doing her own signing. The math integration spilled over into other projects, field trips, and holiday parties. Story time with Barbara Peters and sign language/language-arts vocabulary were their best class times together. They began to mingle, to grow close. Mary Kay found herself bragging about the achievements of her students with disabilities.

But Mary Kay wasn't Kinzie's only regular teacher who was discovering what the special education students could accomplish. Other teachers, students, and parents were learning as well because of Kinzie's Friday Afternoon Activities Program.

I find the Friday Afternoon Activities one of the best ideas Kinzie School has ever had. I like the way Mr. Franklin let us choose the classes we want. It gives us some say in what goes on around here. Furthermore, some of us can use these classes to explore our options, broaden our horizons, get some ideas of which classes we want to take in high school.

What Mr. Franklin wanted to achieve through this program was an added incentive for the students to work hard during the week. He hoped it would increase their level of work academically while ease off on the stress of the work week. I think that Friday Afternoon Activities is a great way to end the week.

Aaron, eighth grade

Friday Afternoon Activities changed that last period of the day on the last day of the week from a dull, down time for cleaning out desks and shooting spit balls to an up, and often exciting, fun experience. Every child in the school picked an activity: basketball, football, volleyball, cheerleading, pompons, or girls' sports. Sewing, cooking, woodworking, nature crafts, puppets, painting, and jewelry making were available for the less athletic. And there was piano, teen talk, computers, Spanish, French culture, sign language, independent science, math enrichment, or yoga. The little kids could participate in scouts, rhythm band, chorus, storytelling, drama, dance, and games. Every Kinzie staff member except the school clerk and the engineer had some activity to lead: teachers, aides, and welfare attendants. Parents took groups, too.

I would like to tell you about our jewelry-making class. We make Indian rings and tissue paper buttons. In our Indian ring we do not use stones or gems; we use

Indian beads. Our next project will be Indian brace-
lets and necklaces. Making jewelry is a lot of fun, and
most girls never have enough jewelry.

Mirrion, learning disabled, seventh grade

You should be a pompon girl because you'll do rap
dances to the music of Vanilla Ice or M. C. Hammer or any
music you pick. You'll make new friends and get new
uniforms. You'll cheer for the basketball team.

Kristin, deaf, fifth grade

I am making Nature Crafts. We will work with all kinds
of things from the outdoors. We already did a project
with leaves. We will be making many other different
things, and they will be nice to give as gifts. I will take
mine home and decorate my room. Maybe I will give some
to my mom.

Luke, communication disorders, seventh grade

I like Spanish. I practice Spanish. Presiliana helps me
read books. Presiliana writes Spanish. She gives me
Spanish papers. Spanish class is fun.

Lucila, hard of hearing, fifth grade

I think you should go to sign language because it is
fun there. You could get a lot of money when you grow
up and be a sign-language teacher.

Gina, second grade

I like to play Steal the Bacon. I like to sell popcorn. In
Cub Scouts we made a balloon race. Cub Scouts pick up
papers and pick up leaves.

Tony, hard of hearing, second grade

Anticipating which activities students might choose, staff members offered to teach classes built on their own skills, interests, and hobbies. Parent expertise and assistance were enlisted through the school newsletter and by word-of-mouth. The Local School Council put some money aside for equipment and supplies and obtained more through a grant from the Fund for Educational Reform. Computer joysticks, a boom box, and miscellaneous supplies were purchased. Stan bought a saw, a sander, and other woodworking tools with award money from the Chicago Foundation for Education. Parents and teachers dug through closets and cabinets for old board games, remnants, and craft supplies. A dedicated group of mothers undertook the Girl Scout Council training and expanded a Brownie troop for hearing and deaf girls, to Daisies, and then Juniors, too.

Employees from the nearby Electro-Motive Division of General Motors (EMD) linked themselves to Kinzie through the Adopt-A-School Program. They began a Career Awareness session for sixth, seventh, and eighth graders. After a firsthand look at the Electro-Motive Division plant and its massive engines, the children participated in a staged emergency that called for first aid know-how and the EMD ambulance and paramedics. Each Friday afternoon different employee teams composed of dieticians, nurses, psychologists, doctors, photographers, and engineers of every kind involved the kids in a presentation on their own occupations.

The Chicago Dance Medium, funded by the Illinois Arts Council, introduced Kinzie to modern dance and created "Always Walk in the Lunchroom Unless Somebody Tells You to Run," a community performance for a Saturday evening in the Kennedy Auditorium. Some of the children, hearing and deaf, later performed in concert with the Chicago Dance Medium in the Fine Arts Building downtown.

I am trying to persuade you to come to dance. We get to dance with special performers. In May there will be a show downtown. We will perform by doing backbends, walking crooked, and high leaps. A lot of people will come to see us. You might become famous.

Clifton, third grade

Donald, a student in the upper-grade severe-learning-disabilities class, eagerly approached his teacher, Mr. Stark, about starting a karate class. After a demonstration session for Mr. Franklin, Donald had the principal's stamp of approval. Kathy Barrett, a special education teacher, volunteered to chaperone his routines. Donald's karate class accumulated a long waiting list of active younger boys.

I think that karate class is interesting, fun, and cool. My opinion is that this class is the one to take! It is interesting because you learn to defend yourself. It is fun because our teacher lets us fight him for thirty seconds. It is cool because we sometimes watch movies.

Daniel, fifth grade

Kinzie's Friday Afternoon Activities offered students with special talents in math, science, gymnastics, or the arts the opportunity to develop those skills. It increased instructional time by consolidating pull-out programs. It gave children a chance to experiment, to try new tasks. It provided a means for using academic skills in real life experiences like woodworking and French culture. It fostered improved social skills by creating an environment for cooperation, interaction, and responsibility. It motivated students to work harder during the week in order to participate in the project of their choice on Friday.

Most significantly and to a greater degree than was ever anticipated, Friday Afternoon Activities integrated children with disabilities. It brought together staff and students who would never have come into contact otherwise. In Friday Afternoon Activities integration of the deaf, communication-disordered, and learning-disabled students became a given. Collaboration between regular and special teachers became natural. Leo, who had always been in self-contained special ed classes, became the star of the basketball team and in June was voted "cutest boy graduate" by all of the eighth graders. Markeeta and Kristin became cheerleaders, Shadarryl leapt across the stage in the Fine Arts Building, James and Brenton choreographed their own basketball dance, Sergio received the Musicianship Award, Donald became a leader, Jennifer and Beth became best friends.

CHAPTER 18

E - I - E - I - O! E - I - E - I - O!
Come on Kinzie Cougars! Let's go!
Scoobee doobee doo! Oh! Oh! Oh! Go! Go! Go!

Jennifer and Beth were very close—not like two peas in a pod— more like corn flakes and cream. Beth was the smooth surface, still quiet, the foil for snappy, crackly Jenni. With her button nose and chestnut hair cut in a mushroom style, Beth was tall for sixth grade. Jennifer by contrast was petite, with porcelain features and a ponytail. The girls were cheerleaders together, showing off in their new, white Kinzie sweatshirts with the grinning, blue cougars charging across the front and their tiny, pleated skirts made for twirling. They cheered at all the home games and even got to travel with the team to one away game. They both had the same favorite cheer: E-I-E-I-O! Energetically, they clapped and jumped and tumbled into the splits, accompanied by the screaming shouts of their enthusiastic classmates. Neither of the girls was upset that the team won only one game. The excitement of the competition was fun enough, and it was Kinzie's first year for basketball.

Jennifer and Beth each had to wake up at dawn's early light to make the band practice promptly at 8:00 each morning. They each played the flute in the advanced band and were rewarded with the special privilege of attending the Chicago Symphony Orchestra Young Performers Concert downtown. They were a nervous pair in their uniform, white blouses and black skirts, when they played in concert for the District Academic Olympics.

In science Jennifer and Beth were lab partners, and they collaborated on a project for the school science fair demonstrating the orbits of the planets. Beth wrote a story about Kinzie's bowling league for the school newspaper, and Jenni had some of her poems and a book review published in the *Kaleidoscope*. Both Jenni and Beth worried about social studies. They had tons of reading to do, and always an enormous number of facts to memorize. Sometimes, they exchanged answers across the room using sign language. They both aimed for the honor roll, and they both were thinking about becoming teachers of deaf children when they grew up. And one other thing they had in common was their crush on Venancio, in eighth grade, who they agreed was the cutest boy in the school.

Beth was a good signer. She had started in Ms. Brownell's class in third grade, and now she enjoyed using her signs to help the little preschool deaf children get ready for dismissal. She especially liked interpreting songs and poems when her class participated in the many seasonal assemblies. Between classes she loved to chat with Jenni.

Jenni began sign with the first flutter of her eyelids. She snuggled into the soft, enveloping world of dancing hands, surrounded by her loving parents and grandparents. Jenni's mother, Patti, and her dad, Bob, were deaf. And Jenni's maternal grandparents were deaf also.

Jenni was the third generation to attend deaf classes in the Chicago public schools. During her grandparents' time the city offered a strictly oral program at Parker elementary and high schools on the south side. Childhood sweethearts, her grandmother and her grandfather never learned sign language until as adults they joined the deaf club. Jenni's grandfather had excellent speech and a good job as a printer for the *Chicago Tribune*. Her grandmother worked at the Harris

Bank until her daughter Patti was born. Then her focus changed to raising her two children, first Patti and then Larry, born twelve years after Patti and hard of hearing. Their parents taught them English at home, mouthing the words for everything in sight even as they signed. Patti and Larry moved easily from sign to English to sign, comfortable communicating in two languages.

Just as her parents before her, Patti attended Chicago public school classes for deaf children, and as in her parents' time, the oral philosophy prevailed. She and her classmates might startle to a tap across the fingers if they lapsed into communicating with their hands because all information was to be absorbed through speechreading and residual hearing. Challenged by her lessons but determined to succeed, Patti performed so well in her deaf classes that she was advanced to a hard of hearing room.

As the year progressed, Patti and her classmates found their assignments increasingly more difficult to understand. Their teacher explained the stories in their traditional reading series orally; speechreading was their only means of deciphering passages or analyzing themes. Constantly frustrated and finally overwhelmed, Patti carried her reader home one evening and asked her dad to help her with her homework. First they read the selection in English together; then her father signed the story to her in American Sign Language (ASL). It was a revelation. The characters, plot, and theme suddenly had meaning. Patti actually enjoyed the story.

The next day she was the only student in her class to answer correctly the twenty comprehension questions listed on the blackboard. Her score of 100 percent so surprised her teacher that she accused Patti of cheating in some way. Flushed with embarrassment, hurt and frightened, Patti explained about the help from her dad; but the teacher just wouldn't believe her. Patti's father was forced to come to school to prove that he had interpreted the story for his daughter. Although the teacher finally acknowledged that Patti's dad had communicated the text to her, she never could fathom the notion that because of his using sign language, Patti really understood the story.

When she graduated from eighth grade, Patti went away to St. John's High School in Milwaukee. Feeling terribly homesick, she drew close to her nineteen deaf classmates who, like her, were anxious about being far from their families for the first time. Patti easily slipped into conversational fluency in sign, and she soaked up the content of courses presented in total communication. In the shelter of the sturdy campus buildings and the half-light of the dormitory residence halls, she began to share with her new friends all the fears and dreams of adolescence. These twenty classmates bonded into inseparable companions, a solid network that in later years, despite geographical separation and diverse experiences, would provide support in times of trouble and misfortune. And these friends would continue to celebrate and congratulate one another in times of accomplishment and joy. At St. John's, with its enrollment of almost 250 deaf students, its deaf teachers, and deaf dorm monitors, Patti entered the world of deaf culture.

After St. John's came Gallaudet University. Patti had grown into a graceful and attractive young woman. Her dark eyes sparkled in contrast to her fair and flawless skin, and she had the high cheek bones and the sharp features of a model. She felt enthusiastic about becoming a teacher or a school counselor, but Gallaudet was more challenging than St. John's and much farther away from her home. And Bob was there. Before her junior year, Patti decided to take a break, to come back to Chicago. She began to work in a bank, and so did

Bob. They never returned to Gallaudet, for two years later they were married.

Patti and Bob anticipated the birth of their first child with the usual new parents' wonder and worry. In addition though, they were unsure if their baby would be hearing or deaf. Bob had lost his hearing through scarlet fever. Patti's very first question to the doctor in the delivery room was "Is she deaf?" The doctor clapped his hands and when Jenni startled, he pronounced her "hearing." Eighteen months later, however, Patti could see that Jenni was deaf. The audiologist confirmed her suspicion, saying Jenni's loss was profound. Patti was deeply depressed. She had been believing for almost two years that Jenni could hear, that Jenni's life would be easier than her own. Now, she was worried about Jenni's future.

It was Patti's mother who consoled her. She gently signed, "Don't be upset; we are all deaf. It will be all right." And Patti accepted that it was true. Jenni was bright and curious and totally lovable. She was forever toddling along, her "cherish" blanket in one hand, Patti's hand in her other. Patti loved sharing the world with her. She and Bob used sign and English, just as Patti's parents had done. They moved their lips and their fingers. Jenni's grandparents used English with Jenni too, as comfortably as they had with Patti. And her Uncle Larry, who had been mainstreamed in regular classes, spoke in English.

Jenni sat with her storybooks for hours, pretending to decode the mysterious letters under the pictures. The books were just like their captioned TV, images framed by lines of puzzling characters. And there was the telecommunication device for the deaf (TDD) on which her mother and father frequently tapped similar curious messages. They smiled or frowned at the machine and then translated for Jenni the news from her uncle, grandparents, or family friends. A secure child, not shy, Jenni lingered with her parents' visitors. She watched their signs with concentration. She was maturing quickly.

Jenni had lots of playmates in the neighborhood. She became acquainted easily, moved confidently, was eager to try novel toys, to experience new adventures. She had good speech and a knack for speechreading. When the time came, Patti enrolled her in the Kinzie preschool program where Jenni's lessons were taught in total communication. Times had changed.

Because Jenni had good speech, her teachers emphasized oral skills. She was an excellent speechreader. She wore her hearing aids religiously and benefited from them. Audiological testing now placed her loss in the severe range. Adjusting to school was a snap for Jenni. She made friends with her classmates quickly and was almost always the leader in her group. She was teacher's pet, encouraged by everyone to achieve, rewarding them when she succeeded.

Jenni could do the extras. She was a member of the first kindergarten communication arts class where she and a hearing partner made colorful crepe paper puppets and signed and sang a rainbow of songs. In second grade she was mainstreamed for reading, and she made the first reading group.

At first Patti was worried that the mainstream classroom might be too much for Jenni, but it wasn't. She was always able to do her homework without Patti's help. Even as she progressed through the grades and the subject matter became more difficult, Jenni mastered it. She stayed on the honor roll. Library, music, computers, art, then math, and finally, all subjects were taught to her in the mainstream.

Patti was pleased with Jenni's academic accomplishments. She viewed Kinzie's educational program firsthand when she came to the school herself to work as a teacher aide. She felt reassured seeing Jenni participating in her classes. She felt comfortable working where she was the third deaf person to be hired as a teacher aide, and where there was a deaf teacher on the staff as well.

Right on my shoulder
is a sleeping lady bug
dreaming about me.

Jennifer, sixth grade

In fifth grade Jennifer won first place in Chicago's citywide deaf spelling bee. The following year she came in second in the Kinzie School spelling bee, second against the hearing students as well as the deaf. In sixth grade Jenni's haiku poem was selected for publication in a special anthology published by Japan Airlines. More than fourteen thousand poems were submitted from around the world, and of these only sixty were chosen.

But in sixth grade Jenni first experienced the rival tugs of her two cultures. Jenni was the only deaf girl mainstreamed all day in the sixth grade. She met her deaf friends in gym, computers, art, and music, but the only time she had to gossip with them was lunch. She missed the cozy companionship of her deaf friends. Yet, Jenni didn't want to give up the challenge of her mainstream class. She was competing, and she was succeeding. She felt that she was an equal to the hearing girls. And she did have Beth for a best friend between classes. But after school she went back to her neighborhood where she no longer had close hearing friends. Her deaf friends were miles away, and she didn't have the time or a place to make new friends near her home.

Jenni complained to Patti. Sometimes, the hearing girls at school were friendly and other times they acted as if she wasn't even there. For no reason, they would ignore her, not talk to her, and she didn't know why. She asked Patti to explain this rude behavior of some of her classmates.

Patti sympathized with Jenni but said she would just have to learn to cope with the situation because the same thing had happened to her when she was a teen. She had felt the same kind of hurt and loneliness at Jenni's age. She had tried to keep those feelings hidden inside herself, too, just as Jenni was doing now.

But Patti told Jenni that she saw the sparkle in her eyes when they attended deaf get-togethers with family or friends. She could see that Jenni enjoyed every moment of these parties and never became bored or lonesome. In high school Jenni could go to ISD, the Illinois state school for the deaf. Jenni would find good friends there, as Patti had at St. John's. Jenni would be a member of sports teams, activities, and clubs with other deaf teens, and she would have a social life that would make her feel accepted in the deaf culture. There would be more opportunities to make friends at ISD than in a hearing high school. It was too difficult to be close to hearing girls. Patti knew the frustration firsthand. Jenni would feel more comfortable in deaf culture. It was their world.

CHAPTER 19

Do you have a dream school? Would $250,000 buy it? Nabisco wants to give some school with a staff like ours the money to create a school that works.

G. Banks

Reform had started with a bang! And a bong. The Interim Board cut more than 500 jobs from the central administration and shifted another 600 positions to the field. These employees now answered directly to local school principals. Jane Blatt left the system when numerous coordinator and supervisor positions were eliminated. Frances Woods became a principal of a small school far away from Kinzie. Ms. Altschuler quietly took her vacation and extended it ad infinitum. She had finally retired. No one replaced her. District 10 swallowed up Districts 18 and 19, and half of the city's district superintendents were given the choice of retiring or becoming principals. A few even settled for substitute teacher positions. It was a topsy turvy traumatic time for many board employees who had served the Chicago system all of their professional lives.

A new director of special education was appointed. Dr. Thomas Hehir had heard about Chicago's problems way back in Boston, and still he was optimistic when he met with Mr. Franklin in the fall of 1990. He admitted that he was dumbfounded by the board's denial of speech services to deaf children, and at that very moment he was in the process of signing a consent decree concerning the provision of speech instruction. Furthermore, he was determined to recruit a number of speech pathologists who were also knowledgeable about deaf education. Although his main philosophical thrust would be *inclusion*, in the area of deafness, he felt a certain critical mass of students was necessary in order to have a viable program. He did not intend to advocate that all deaf children be returned to their home schools.

He felt there was indeed a need for more case managers, and he was fully aware of the lack of auditory-training equipment and audiologists. He couldn't believe that there was no money designated in a specific budget line for amplification. He couldn't believe that for years there were no interpreters provided to the elementary schools. Dr. Hehir was bringing in a consultant from Boston to provide both a philosophy and programmatic guidelines for the deaf program in Chicago. He felt that the system was on the move and not just turning upside down.

The closing of the District 18 offices was a boon for Kinzie because it made six new rooms available for classes. They only had to be cleared out first. Nobody wanted the records in the district file cabinets, but the cabinets themselves were in high demand. Hundreds of garbage bags were dragged to the alley before all of the district principals filed through and initialed their furniture and equipment selections. Then we Kinzie staff members picked over the leavings. I confiscated Ms. Altschuler's great, green, glass bowl of paper clips and a real treasure of a scratch pad imprinted "From the desk of Ms. Altschuler." What trepidation had been stirred up in the past by the flutter of one of those green notes.

The Kinzie Local School Council decided to focus its attention on early education. Having vacant rooms made it possible for our school to get a state-sponsored prekindergarten program for young hearing children at risk. Council members voted to change our kindergarten from a half-day to a full-time session and to decrease class size in first and second grades. Chapter 1 money, extra state funds for low-income students, bought another teacher; and consequently, more children with disabilities could be mainstreamed more readily.

Everyone was breathing freely now. Big Sister was gone, all the Big Sisters and Big Brothers—gone. Kinzie was on its own. Faculty members created committees to develop a Next Century Schools grant application. Our biggest concerns were early education, parenting, staff development, team teaching, and mainstreaming. In small groups, teachers and parents proposed their ideal programs.

Some envisioned a Parent Center staffed by a teacher, social worker, nurse, preschool aide, and parent volunteers, a welcoming environment where moms and dads could browse through a book, toy, and video library. It would look and feel like a home and include the facilities for modeling positive parenting skills. Teenage parents who needed direction in meal planning, fostering good health habits, and disciplining misbehavior could find help in this center. They could also learn how to encourage language development with their toddlers. With instruction, parents could practice saying, "oo-ee" or making a twisting, cookie-cutter motion, and then provide a chocolate chip snack to reward their child's imitation of the sound or movement. They would discover how to modify pudgy fingers pointing to a refrigerator door into the udder milking motion of real sign language.

Other teachers looked to the Parent Center as an opportunity for presenting prevocational skills. Some students in the communication-disorders and deaf classes needed real-life practical experience in self-help and survival skills.

Another group planned for after-school tutoring and a homework center manned by volunteers. Arts and crafts and sports could be offered for the first time to the children with disabilities; activity buses would be provided to take them home in the late afternoon.

Some teachers suggested innovative scheduling to encourage more team teaching, peer observation, and peer coaching. There could be shared planning time, shared expertise, and Kinzie's own teachers acting as instructional leaders. Regular and special education students could be taught together in a variety of groupings.

President Next Century Schools Fund
RJR Nabisco Foundation

Our Next Century Schools application was developed with input from well over half of our school's staff. When we initially received the application, we placed a notice on the counter in our school office inviting interested teachers to an informational meeting. At that meeting we asked teachers to provide us with their vision of the kind of programs and activities that would exist in their "dream school."

The response of the staff was immediate, thoughtful, and enthusiastic. This proposal is the end result of that collaborative effort. It was done by a staff which I am extremely proud of.

James P. Franklin

Kinzie didn't receive a Next Century Schools Grant. The school wasn't awarded $250,000 or any money from Nabisco. Nevertheless, some of the plans developed during the application process were initiated. In small steps the programs that cost little or nothing were started. The Local School Council (LSC) voted funds for after-school math tutoring, bought a full-time social worker, a full-time art teacher. And because of these grant-development meetings, a few more parents and staff members became less hesitant to reach out to others, less reluctant to try something different. Teachers accustomed to presenting lessons with their doors closed, left them open a crack.

Parents of hearing children who were helping with Friday Afternoon Activities found that they wanted to communicate with the deaf children in their groups themselves, instead of always relying on an interpreter. They joined with parents of deaf children to participate in the ongoing Wednesday sign-language classes.

The board assigned one interpreter to Kinzie School. There was a genuine need for three, but Joanne Napier was welcomed heartily. Joanne was Beth's sister; so we now had the sister of our deaf teacher aide and the mothers of two deaf students interpreting. Donna and Veda continued to serve in academic classes and at band practice. Child-welfare attendants still accompanied the deaf classes in mainstreamed gym to translate directions and game rules, and they began to monitor the lunchroom, which had become totally integrated. Traditionally, teachers of the deaf had been required to eat lunch with their homerooms, but regular classroom teachers were free. Now all of Kinzie's teachers could become better acquainted over a tuna sandwich or tossed salad while their kids gestured back and forth in the burrito line.

And deaf children were mainstreamed into the upper grades, a place where the junior high teachers said they would never be. Marilyn Steiner accompanied the group of deaf children who were ready for sixth-grade math skills.

I went to 229 room. Suddenly, I looked math test paper is not easy, might difficulty. I want try to work. Mr.

Krenshaw call five minutes, hurry up! I get quickly work
math test. I think maybe C or D+ math test.

Kenith, deaf, sixth grade

Marilyn first served as an interpreter for her six deaf students. Gradually, subtly, she eased into the role of a team
teacher reinforcing concepts in a visual way. Charts and dia-
grams were sparse in the math room. Almost adjacent to the
ceiling was a lone border of famous quotations, which had
faded into the north wall. If the students strained their heads
back far enough and their eyes forward enough, they might
decipher the pronouncements of Aristotle, Plato, Newton,
and Einstein extolling the value of education. Centered on the
south wall was a dusky, gray computer banner, a brittle ad-
monition that "Knowledge Is Power." A few dusty cones and
pyramids dating from the age of Cheops dangled in one corner, while in another, the remnant of a faded flag first
mounted in the year that Mr. Krenshaw came to Kinzie hung
limply from its staff. The math teacher would not accept a
new flag to replace it; hence, Alaska and Hawaii were still
awaiting their admittance to the union here.

Marilyn prepared charts when the deaf students needed
them. As she tutored those who were having difficulty, she
discovered which simple illustrations could make a difference. She began to stick up her charts on the math teacher's
blank bulletin boards, lively rectangles of color in the bland
surroundings.

Mr. Krenshaw did use the blackboards; he filled them with
figures from top to bottom, then began a second layer. The
students blinked with bewilderment as the background and
numbers became one dusty blur. They whispered to each
other in disbelief as the chalk disappeared into grains of

dust, and still Mr. Krenshaw continued writing with his empty fingers.

Ms. Steiner unobtrusively dragged an eraser down the ledge pushing the dust into the waiting wastebasket in the corner. When the math teacher was absent from his room, she sent a student in to wash the boards. She placed fresh sticks of chalk along the clean ledge. She supplemented the short supply of rulers and protractors and replaced the broken compasses. Because of Marilyn's persistence the children learned by looking and touching as well as by listening, thinking, and writing.

It was a tough year, but the kids passed. Surprising himself, Kenith earned a B and Sergio even got an A. Sergio frequently managed to score the highest grade in the class. And perhaps the visual learners among the hearing students were helped by the charts that, in any case, brought a little color to Einstein's cheeks.

Mr. Krenshaw always has spots of chalk on his pants. He is tall, wears glasses, and is as thin as a toothpick. When we go to his class and go over the work, and we are talking or not paying attention, he will call on us to see if someone else's problem is right. He will give us a brand new problem, and if we get it wrong, he will say, "It's a good thing your mother or father isn't here to see you in action."

Juan, sixth grade

As long as the deaf students kept up, Mr. Krenshaw could accept them as appropriate members of his class. He was willing to take his students as far as they would go, and every year he had a few eighth graders that he tutored in high-school algebra. They met at 8:30 A.M., a half-hour before school, on alternate days of the week. Mr. Krenshaw had a tradition of winning Math Counts teams and an exemplary record at the Academic Olympics. He congratulated Sergio for his high test scores, often lauding his progress in front of the entire class.

It was remarkable that Sergio had persevered to full-time mainstreaming in sixth grade. He had begun with Jenni and six other deaf five-year-olds in the kindergarten communication arts class, but he was the quietest child in the group. In temperament Jenni's exact opposite, Sergio tagged along with her to second-grade reading, but he needed to be coaxed to recite. A bashful boy whose speech was not as intelligible as Jenni's, he hesitated to communicate with the teacher or his classmates. Even with a powerful hearing aid, Sergio discriminated no speech. At home he heard only the indistinct rolling cadences of Spanish, no English to reinforce his school language lessons. But Sergio watched intently. His large, brown eyes, beaming from beneath the umbrage of his shaggy, ebony bangs, always focused on the teacher, on the central activity of the lesson.

In third-grade reading, Sergio persisted, silent as the sphinx. But Glor, his teacher that year, loved to teach speech; and using Sergio's reading vocabulary and phonics lessons, she multiplied the number of words he could articulate. He was an excellent speechreader, and his speech was at last emerging.

When Sergio moved to fourth grade, his homeroom teacher, Barb Ridgeway, interpreted reading instruction for him and Jenni for two periods each day. She feared that, bright as Sergio was, he just might be too sensitive to succeed against the increasing pressures of mainstreaming. Every teacher noted his timidity and attempted to bolster his confidence in one way or another. Tentative as a tortoise and just as tenacious, he plodded on through reading, communication arts, gym, art, library, computers, and music. Weighed down by his shell of seriousness, only occasionally did Sergio slip into a smile.

Music sparked that smile. Despite the severity of his hearing loss, Sergio enjoyed music class. Drawing up all his courage, he even auditioned for the band and started playing the saxophone. To the amazement of Janine Patenkin, Kinzie's music teacher and band director, Sergio successfully performed a solo in 6/8 time his first year. While his classmates were still counting 4/4 time, he moved on to more complex rhythms. Janine had used a mathematical approach with Sergio, and he grasped the idea immediately.

Then, for Friday Afternoon Activities, Sergio chose piano. One day when his group, made up of hearing children, was struggling with page five of the instruction booklet, Sergio advanced by himself to page twenty-two. He adjusted for the flats, naturals, and fingerings all on his own. That year he won Kinzie's "Outstanding Musicianship Award." By fifth grade Sergio had band practice every morning, a saxophone sectional for forty minutes, and an hour of piano on Fridays.

I love woodwinds because of the feeling of breathing life into the instrument. I'm learning how to connect the pitch and quality of the note with the feeling I get from the sax. It's not as sensitive as hearing, but it's possible for me to recognize a good note.

James Canning, deaf saxophonist

"It's the brain, not the ear that is used for music." In company with Sergio, there were twelve deaf kids, one child with communication disorders, and three severe-learning-disabilities students in the fifty-member Kinzie Band. Kenith, who was absolutely stone deaf, the only child in the department who never wore a hearing aid, played the drums. The B in math made it possible. Janine said she needed a drummer who could count, and Kenith could count. But Kenith had an intense feeling for music. With his hands implanted on the stereo speakers, he concentrated his eyes on the fingers of the interpreter, trying to capture the nuances of emotion that Ms. Patenkin described during music class. Kenith wanted to feel each concerto, sonata, and symphonic movement as the composer had. Sergio had that same fervor. Timidly, he told Janine that he would like to write his own music, to be a composer himself some day, but then he seemed to take it back. It was too much to expect.

Sergio's family didn't expect too much either. He was their baby of five children, and they all accepted, supported, and sheltered him. Some of Sergio's quiet persistence was rooted in his family. They were close-knit: his mother, a homemaker, his father, a packer in a meat-packing company, and his four older brothers and sisters. All signed a little. All attended Catholic church together.

Sergio was a good boy at home. He took responsibility for his own belongings and for helping around the house. He didn't mind cleaning up in the kitchen or emptying the garbage. He liked to mow the lawn. He didn't have any friends in the neighborhood, didn't venture very far from his front door. He watched TV with his father after his sister and brother helped him with his homework. Sergio was closest to Rosa, who signed the most. Sometimes he enjoyed drawing pictures with his little cousins, and he shared his love of music with his older brother Victor. They played duets on the saxophone and guitar. Sergio continued with Confraternity of Christian Doctrine classes at a church where sign language was used.

Family Stories
When I was about one year old, my family and I went to Brookfield Zoo. My sister put me on a stone bench because my father wanted to take my picture. The camera made a big flash that hurt my eyes. I fell in the mud. I got all sloppy and had mud all over me! My father couldn't take my picture because I was all dirty.

Sergio, deaf, fifth grade

Sergio shared this story with his classmates in fifth-grade communication arts class. He read it to them, and he was only a little shy about it. They laughed along with him because they all had their own embarrassing stories to tell that week.

The following month the students paired up and interviewed each other. They took turns photographing themselves in twos and threes, adopting silly poses and even wearing wild outfits concocted from leftover costumes in the assembly box. They all relaxed and had a good time together.

Sergio is ten years old and his favorite color is sky blue. On weekends Sergio likes to play with his Legos. On a hot summer day, he would prefer cherry or strawberry Kool-Aid. When he grows up, he would like to be a well-educated banker. Sergio's favorite subjects in school are music and art. After school he likes to take a short nap and then do his homework.

Anika, sixth grade

Sergio's participation in the arts strengthened his self-confidence. Young Authors was an annual activity in communication arts. In second grade Sergio dictated a delightful picture book about two duck friends sharing the playground swings, slide, and pond, then waddling home. In third grade he snipped his scary storybook into the shape of a witch's ugly face with a protruding nose and scraggly hair. Sergio was the first deaf child to have his book submitted to the District Young Authors committee. As the years progressed, he blended his imagination and experience into essays, poems, and more storybooks.

If I were little like Tom Thumb, I would ride on a paper airplane or in a toy car. I could use an ant for a pet. I would play baseball with a toothpick and a pea. I would take a bath in a cup. A cotton ball would be my pillow, and my mother would cut me a tiny blanket. I would sleep in my brother's shoe. I would be happy because my mother would take care of me and hug me.

Sergio, deaf, fifth grade

In sixth grade Sergio felt comfortable at last in contemplating the stars—even in following his own star. Surprisingly, it turned out to be within his reach, a firefly in the fold of his sleeve.

> Light that twinkles slow
> blinks at every night and
> twinkles at dawn too.
>
> Sergio, deaf, sixth grade

CHAPTER 20

The John H. Kinzie School is fully committed to a mainstreaming policy which will result in every student being given
the opportunity to realize his/her full potential. This policy
is grounded in the law, which states that each special education student is entitled to a free and appropriate education in
the least restrictive environment.

I n August teachers and parents got together for two days of
planning; mainstreaming was one of the major topics for
discussion. Teachers volunteered their time; the reward
was a treat from the LSC and Mr. Franklin, lunch at Sharkos
restaurant where the chicken Caesar salad was a faculty favorite. Even though they were payless days, 85 percent of the
staff attended.

Mr. Franklin increased class membership in a few cases by
one student and managed to create an opening for a school
mainstream coordinator. Gloria Strablenka was selected for
the position. Glor had probably had the greatest number of
students over the years mainstreamed from her own deaf
classes into regular reading. She had dealt with her students'
frustrations, diagnosed their common problems, and discovered some adjustments teachers could make to promote success in the regular classroom. She had, on more than one
occasion, suggested the need for a mainstream resource person on the staff.

It was Glor's job to serve as liaison between regular and
special ed teachers. She would assist them in making mainstreaming decisions: selecting students, deciding which personnel would be involved, and what subjects taught. She was

not to dictate arrangements but to foster cooperative decisions among the staff.

One of her biggest headaches was setting up an interpreter schedule to cover all of the students now mainstreamed at every level. The board was still not sending interpreters. Any teacher of the deaf might be called on to interpret during a free period if it was one of those days when more than one interpreter was absent. No one was burdened by it, though, because there were enough teachers to go around and most found it an enlightening experience. Joey's mother, Shelly, enrolled in an interpreter training program.

Glor also served as a resource for mainstreamed students and monitored the deaf children's progress. She took her job seriously, stopping kids in the lunchroom or the halls regularly to find out how they were doing, if they were having any problems. Joey and Shadarryl were slipping in science. She talked to Steve, their third-grade teacher, and arranged to tutor them herself. She made sure that every classroom with mainstream students had an overhead projector. She met with parents of mainstreamed students to urge them to check their children's homework and spend a little extra time if needed so that their kids kept up with their hearing classmates. She reminded teachers about preferential seating and the use of the FM system. She prodded them about visual learning techniques, and she sent them "thank you–good job" notes.

Kinzie's mainstreaming program was becoming a kaleidoscope of shifting teacher-student collaborations. Glor interpreted in Linda Winters's first-grade class for four deaf students, and then she tutored them in her resource room for one period each day. She invited their parents to visit and observe in both rooms. They were in the middle of their porcupine story, and Shannon's and Tova's moms marveled at the various prickly creatures housed in the Room 102 Zoo.

The children had combined pretzels, toothpicks, twigs, and straight pins with oranges, styrofoam, and clay to create a porcupine menagerie.

Michaelle Brownell, a second-generation teacher who had the other first-grade class, teamed with Maureen Brongly, who brought her deaf students into Michaelle's room for Junior Great Books. First, they read a story together; then, they dramatized it in their makeshift costumes or class-made masks. Finally, they talked about it in total communication.

Later in the day Kathy Barrett ushered into Michaelle's classroom a line of her primary children with communication disorders. It was time for intensive phonics. No one could tell which class was Kathy's or which was Michaelle's as they merged into one class at the chalkboard, racing to write their vowel exercises and then enthusiastically erasing them away with their old socks.

In third grade Joey and Shadarryl were mainstreamed with interpreters for reading and science. Glor provided tutoring as the need arose, and it did on several occasions. Mary Kay Sandusky and Barbara Ridgeway had become a team, teaching deaf and hearing students a variety of fifth-grade subjects together. Sergio and Jenni were fully included in all sixth-grade classes with an interpreter.

Barb and Julie continued their deaf awareness program for kindergarten children and all of Kinzie's transfer students. Every class in the school had sign language once each week. Hearing students were becoming fluent enough to sign their science fair reports for the deaf children visiting the exhibits. Signing often stirred silent classrooms when talking was prohibited. In between the subtests of the Illinois Goals Assessment, I watched hearing students relaxing and chatting in sign to one another during the five-minute breaks. And I saw giant signs spanning a hallway or the lunchroom.

In the spring of that school year, Kinzie received the board of education packet "Inclusive Schools Project." It opened with the following statement:

An appreciation of diversity and forming meaningful relationships are two important reasons for choosing public education for students with disabilities. Removing these children from a traditional setting deprives all students of the opportunity to know and benefit from the talents and gifts of a significant number of their peers, and to appreciate their needs. In the city of Chicago, one in every nine or ten children has a disability; about one in a hundred has a disability that impacts them severely in daily life. Going to school with a group of children who reflect this reality can teach powerful lessons to tomorrow's leaders. Integrating persons with disabilities in housing, employment, recreation, transportation, and other domains is ensured by federal law. It is a worthwhile effort, and our schools must acknowledge and plan for the implementation of this well-established social policy.

The board had completely reversed its philosophy of special education. It moved from two completely separate systems directly to one inclusive educational program. Mainstreaming, which never had made it *in,* was now *out.* The policy was *inclusion,* and in the Chicago Public Schools it was defined as an *attempt to paint a vision.*

We can recall the struggle throughout childhood and adolescence to be included, not excluded; to be accepted, not rejected; to be invited, not isolated. Inclusion is a belief that all children have the same needs for acceptance, friendships and connectedness. It is a belief that we need to return to one educational system for all students; that all students are regarded as rightful members of the class and school; and that each and every student be provided instructional curriculum to meet their individual needs and learning styles.

Two major principles were listed for successful inclusion programs: home school placement and noncategorical, individualized service delivery.

This means that students should be served, as much as possible, within the schools they would attend if they were not disabled and should be provided with individualized programs that meet their needs. In smaller schools, cross-categorical positions will be the primary option. In larger schools, the configuration of the special education department is a local option, so long as the school maintains staff capable of implementing the students' IEPs.

Kinzie was named one of Chicago's Inclusive Schools Project models. Severe and profound hearing disabled children were still being regarded as unique, requiring a critical mass of students to generate an appropriate program. They were not members of the first wave of children with disabilities targeted to be removed from their special education classes and returned to their home schools.

Every Kinzie teacher received a copy of the Mainstreaming Policy, and almost all felt comfortable with it.

Mainstreaming will be implemented whenever it is determined at a multidisciplinary conference that a child will benefit at least as much academically from a mainstreamed environment as he/she would from a special education class. Factors such as socialization, peer acceptance, and self-esteem will be considered in making this judgment, but they will be secondary as the primary purpose of schooling is the development of cognitive ability.

We consider it appropriate for the regular education teacher to make adjustments and adaptations in order to include the special education child. Those adjustments will include, but will not be limited to, things like individualized instruction, accommodation for a visual learning style, peer tutoring, utilization of ancillary resources, and collaboration and consultation with the special education teacher, the mainstream facilitator, and the team leader. The extent to which adjustments and adaptations are implemented will be governed by the precept that no changes or modifications may legitimately be implemented which would result in a dilution of the level of instruction which is provided to all the students in the class.

J. Franklin

Kinzie offered a picture of its mainstreaming program to all of Illinois's teachers of deaf students at the ITHI conference in Springfield, "Illinois's Best—1992." Mr. Franklin, Ms.

Brownell, Glor, Mary Kay, and I presented a panel discussion that highlighted our school's growth against the historical background of deaf education. We included our struggles and our successes. We included the nuts and bolts of building an integrated educational program, and we included the divergent perspectives of both special and regular teachers. In addition, we included the dangers involved in isolating deaf children in their home schools without the support they need to succeed, the dangers of *inclusion*.

CHAPTER 21

The misinterpretation of PL 94–142 that promotes main-streaming as the most appropriate and least restrictive environment has placed and continues to place the appropriate and successful education of the Deaf child in jeopardy. If this misinterpretation continues, by the end of the century an entire generation of Deaf children will have been sacrificed to the gods of educational and legislative ignorance!

Jess Freeman King, Ed.D.,
The Bicultural Center News

For one week in 1988, *Gallaudet* became a household word. Deaf college students had drawn major television networks to their Washington, D.C., campus by closing it down. More than one thousand striking deaf students marched to the university board of directors' meeting, then on to the White House, and finally, to the Capitol. Proclaiming a message of Deaf Pride, their posters read, "We still have a dream." That dream became embodied in the demand that a deaf person head Gallaudet, the only accredited liberal arts university in the world primarily for deaf students. But the chair of Gallaudet's board of directors had answered their demand with the condescending and paternalistic statement that "the deaf are not yet ready to function in the hearing world."

In response, students from the National Technical Institute for the Deaf (NTID) in Rochester, New York, and deaf people from all parts of the country poured onto the Gallaudet campus, their capital and center of deaf culture. They came to demonstrate for the dignity of their deafness, and they gathered to put an end to the benevolent caretaker attitude that had become synonymous with the institution. They regarded their own deafness as a difference, not a disability. They championed the striking student leaders and supported their four demands: first, the chair of the board must resign immediately; second, the new president of the university must be deaf; third, the new board of directors must include a 51 percent majority of deaf members; and fourth, there must be no reprisals for student actions.

Their dream became a reality. I. King Jordan, a deaf member of the Gallaudet faculty, was named president. It was a victory for all deaf people. A tiny minority, just .2 percent of the population, had focused the attention of 99.8 percent of the population, hearing Americans, on the raising of deaf consciousness. Kinzie students watched the college demonstrations on TV. They witnessed deaf people dramatically assuming responsibility for their own self-determination. Deaf and hearing children both could read the signs of deaf power and deaf pride. They looked at the deaf people in their own school building, Barbara, Beth, and Patti, but they had little interaction with them. All three women still concentrated the majority of their efforts on clerical responsibilities.

Terry Kennedy, Kinzie's first deaf teacher, arrived in 1990. He was assigned as a cadre substitute, which meant that he was here on a daily basis and worked with all of the deaf classes one day or another. Terry brought a new and inspirational dimension to the language of sign, for he was a talented actor as well as a teacher. Staff and students watched in awe as he vividly dramatized a reading selection or a poem in ASL. In seconds an entire spectrum of emotions flickered across his squarish face, like a silent movie screen reeling into motion. A frame of curly hair softened the picture, but his dark mustache added a touch of mystery. His body was tuned with a spring, and his movements displayed the versatility of Charlie Chaplin. Quiet though he was, there was nothing obscure in his communication. And that was a major concern of Terry's. He introduced the issue of clear signing. He made teachers who were concerned about speech articulation aware that they should also be striving for clearly articulated signing. Sloppy hands and home signs were not satisfactory. For students and teachers he advocated the use of ASL. He hammered at the idiosyncracies, the conceptual confusion involved in signed English.

Kinzie was a total communication school, signing English—not exact English, but pidgin—a combination of ASL signs with English sentence structure. Terry pinpointed frequent examples in the children's texts of passages that translated into absurdity if signed literally in English. On every page of the literature-based readers were idiomatic expressions like "Try hard and keep your eye on the ball." Those few words, "keep your eye on," were so familiar to the hearing children because they had heard them a million times, but they were new to the children who did not hear. When the deaf kids encountered the phrase for the first time in print, the English signs evoked for them a ludicrous picture of an eyeball on the ball. Of course, signing "watch" made more sense than "keep" "your" "eye" "on" "the" "ball." Teachers appreciated the value of conceptually accurate signing immediately. Science, social studies, language arts, health and safety—all types of classes were easier to teach when the presentation was not ambiguous.

Terry argued further for ASL as the first language of the deaf, their natural language. He never used his voice, although he had been taught speech and educated in English himself. Barbara, Beth, and Patti, Kinzie's deaf teacher aides, accommodated their hearing coworkers by using their voices, signing English, and making communication easier. They blended smoothly into the Kinzie mainstream. But Terry signed ASL. He used no lip movements, no spoken sounds unless a communication breakdown occurred. When Terry taught ASL classes for teachers, he allowed no voice interpreting. If necessary, he would write. He felt his students needed to concentrate on watching. ASL is visual; being visual, it is the language most natural for deaf children to learn.

For centuries deaf people hadn't realized that they had a language of their own. Sign was regarded as a vague system of gestures in which each movement imitated in some way the idea it was supposed to represent. It wasn't until the 1950s that William Stokoe theorized that signed languages were natural languages like English, French, or Japanese. Linguists had always assumed that language had to be based on speech, the modulation of sound, but Stokoe argued that sign language was based on the movement of hands, the modulation of space. He had analyzed the signing of his students and found that just like spoken languages, which combine bits of sound, each meaningless by itself, into meaningful words, sign language followed similar rules. It combined individually meaningless hand and body movements into words. Signers began with the choice of a handshape such as a fist or two pointing fingers. They selected a place to make the sign, on the face or possibly the palm of the other hand. They decided how to orient the hand and arm, and then they moved from one part of the body to another or in a particular pattern. Perhaps they began at the hand and finished at the head. Each sign contained four elements: handshape, palm orientation, location, and movement; and the combination of these elements distinguished one sign from another.

In 1960 Stokoe published his book delineating the structure of ASL; this was followed five years later by the first dictionary of American Sign Language. Linguists began to investigate seriously the origins and representations of sign. Everywhere the researchers found deaf people, they observed them using sign language, not the same signs, but fifty different native sign languages worldwide. By the 1980s most linguists had accepted sign language as a natural language, and they had placed it on an equal footing with spoken languages. In addition, scientists had discovered that visual language activity, just like that of spoken languages, was centered in the left brain.

Some educators then began to propose that ASL be used as the language of instruction for all deaf children, and English be taught as a second language for reading and writing. Advocates for the bilingual and bicultural approach argued that language is inseparable from culture. They defined deaf culture as a group of people sharing similar values, outlooks, frustrations, and *sign language*. They further argued for separate classes and schools for the deaf, in direct opposition to the movement for the least-restrictive environment, mainstreaming, and inclusion.

> A situation has been created which is causing more and more Deaf children to be lost educationally, emotionally, and socially. In the name of "inclusion" and "mainstreaming," the Deaf child's linguistic socio-cultural communication and language development needs are often inadequately addressed, if not totally disregarded.
>
> Jess Freeman King

Kinzie had clearly defined its policy of mainstreaming deaf students whenever and wherever it was appropriate. We had gradually modified our programs so that they facilitated *appropriate* mainstreaming. Yet we were beginning to appreciate the relationship of American Sign Language and deaf culture. The use of ASL, however, created a dilemma for Kinzie's mainstreamed classes. American Sign Language can not be communicated simultaneously with spoken English because it mandates turning off your voice. In the communication arts classes, hearing and deaf children had been speaking and signing together for years. Terry substituted in this program, teaming with Marcia, the art teacher, for one full semester. Marcia voice-interpreted for the hearing children, but because Terry used the wonderfully narrative facial expressions and the pantomimic body movements of a trained actor, often it wasn't even necessary.

Terry's major at Gallaudet had been drama. His favorite production in college was the melodramatic, brooding *Macbeth*, yet he was equally comfortable in comedy. After graduation Terry brought his acting skills to the social studies department at St. John's High School for the Deaf in Milwaukee, his own alma mater. However, when St. John's closed down, Terry left teaching to try his luck in Hollywood. After two years in California, he decided that acting full-time was not a full-time-paying profession. He returned to his home in the Midwest.

Terry had been born just outside Chicago, in Elmhurst, the baby of three boys. At the age of six months he suffered through meningitis, losing his hearing to the disease. It was a terrible shock for his mother, and she persevered in seeking a cure for his deafness for many years. First, she took her son to Northwestern University to see Dr. Helmer Myklebust, the recognized leader in research on deafness at that time, the author of numerous textbooks. According to his tests, Terry's hearing loss was *total,* but fortunately, the meningitis had not affected his cognitive abilities. Immediately, Ms. Kennedy began teaching her son speech and language herself. She sent for the famous John Tracy Clinic materials, and she organized an educational regimen in their home. Patiently, she practiced the games and exercises designed to develop spoken language, speechreading, and auditory-training skills.

When Terry turned four, Ms. Kennedy enrolled him in a private, neighborhood preschool where the principal agreed to accept him on the condition that they would keep his deafness a secret. The principal requested this deception out of concern for the parents of the hearing children, who, he felt, might be disturbed by the boy's condition.

Terry was soon also registered in the local public school program for deaf children. There was only one class available so Terry studied with the same teachers for a few years. He learned English and created some homemade signs, but his mother still hoped to somehow reverse his hearing loss. She was even willing to try the power of a faith healer. When that desperate action failed, she finally resigned herself to sending Terry to St. Rita School for the Deaf in Ohio and then to St. John's High School in Milwaukee. His introduction to American Sign Language broadened Terry's world, and later, at Gallaudet, acting classes transformed it. The blend of ASL and drama percolated into the unique teacher Terry became.

In Kinzie's Communication-Arts program, Terry inspired the students to interpret in sign the poems that they had composed in class. The images created in ASL were beautiful representations of their haikus describing flight, but the children had difficulty signing their poems and reciting them in English simultaneously, as they had always done in the past. Because there was not a sign for *word correspondence* in American Sign Language and the order in ASL differed from English word order, it was impossible for the children to sign and to speak simultaneously. For the assembly it was decided to perform in pairs, each with one speaker and one signer. Markeeta was a signing partner. Her graceful movements were a lovely complement to the poem she chose.

Hungry white sea gull
gliding above, lives on the
beach, I throw him food.

Ryan, fifth grade

After the performance, however, Donna expressed her concern that her daughter's speech, which now came naturally, had been stifled by the instruction not to use her voice. Markeeta appeared on stage only signing in ASL. English was Donna's and Markeeta's native language. Donna had fought hard for Markeeta's right to speech services, and Markeeta had proven she could speak clearly and expressively in English. She and her mom wanted her to continue doing so. And that was the hope of most of Kinzie's mothers and fathers. More than 90 percent of the deaf children had hearing parents. English was the language they wanted for their children.

Unfortunately, unlike Markeeta, most of her classmates weren't able to assimilate English completely enough for it to become their native language, and they did not have early access to American Sign Language either. They arrived in school with no real native language. Children whose parents were taking sign classes might have acquired, at most, one hundred signs, compared to their hearing counterparts, who typically entered school with a six-thousand-word vocabulary. Kinzie teachers attempted to teach their deaf students English. Sometimes they were successful; most times they were not.

CHAPTER 22

You'll never fail until you stop trying.
Ms. Cobb-Huston, Kinzie Graduates' Book, 1992

Darren spoke English as well as Markeeta, but he didn't always understand the language he was articulating. Signing in ASL clarified the meaning for Darren. Actually comprehending the message he was communicating enabled Darren to add his personal feelings to his utterances. He became Terry's most attentive pupil, and he learned how to use his entire body as a tool of poetic imagery. Darren's representation of a bird in flight, his performance of the eagle poem, captivated the Kinzie audience and was the highlight of the spring assembly.

Enchanting eagle
swooping down upon our heads
then soaring away.
James, sixth grade

It had taken Darren many years to reach this point of accomplishment, to be able to organize his communications. He no longer stopped David Trainor in the hall with the question, "D. L. today?" reversing even "L. D." Learning-disabilities services were beginning to effect an improvement in Darren's achievement. Being almost hard of hearing, he was one of those children the veterans said were more difficult to teach. Instilling strategies for unraveling jumbled auditory messages was a much more complex process than teaching visually, beginning with almost no aural clues. Darren had, in addition to his auditory problems, learning problems, and a multitude of problems at home. His mom was young, and their project apartment was crowded with active baby brothers and sisters. There was no one in Darren's household with the time or the ability to help reassemble the jigsaw puzzle of his life. School was his only hope.

Kinzie had another struggle in the effort to obtain learning-disabilities service for children like Darren. Pat Bradshaw, the school psychologist, had been documenting deaf students' learning disabilities and offering teachers suggestions for remediating these problems in their classrooms for a long time. Ms. Brownell compiled a list of all of the children Pat had identified, and she enumerated their specific difficulties. When she requested assistance from Jane Blatt, she was told that learning-disabilities remediation, like speech, was the responsibility of the classroom teacher. Mr. Franklin, however, would not allow the matter to be dropped. Hearing children received learning-disabilities services when they needed them; why not the deaf children? Kinzie already had David Trainor, who was trained and certified in deaf education and learning disabilities, assigned to a self-contained deaf classroom. Because of Mr. Franklin's persistence, Jane eventually arranged a part-time learning-disabilities assignment for David at Kinzie. She set up an impossible case load of forty-six students in four schools on the south side of the city. Thanks to Ms. Brownell's documentation, Kinzie had enough students to comprise a reasonable case load and to justify David's services full-time there.

Among David's first identified learning-disabilities students were Darren and Leo. In June of 1992, the same month Darren soared into the assembly firmament, Leo graduated from Kinzie. Leo was one of eleven special education students included in the traditional commencement ceremony for the first time.

Because Leo was one of the stars of the basketball team during Friday Afternoon Activities, he became very popular with the kids in the regular classes. Leo had been in self-contained deaf classes in his earliest years until it was discovered that he was not really deaf. Leo had a problem making sense out of the sounds he heard. It was a central nervous system, auditory processing disability. Leo was therefore transferred to Kinzie's severe-communication-disorders class where he continued to use signs with speech to communicate and to work individually on his learning problems with David. Because he needed intense language remediation, his only mainstreamed classes were gym, music, art, and computers.

When Leo became a basketball star, however, he simultaneously achieved hero status in the lunchroom. He was voted "cutest," "best dressed," and "boy with the best hairstyle" in the graduating class. His prophecy read that he would star as the head munchkin in the remake of the Wizard of Oz. It was a ludicrous joke because Leo was one of the tallest boys in eighth grade. His chiseled Spanish features, long lashes over smiling brown eyes, and stylish appearance drew second looks from all the giggling teenage girls.

Along with Leo, ten other students with special needs were included in the graduation ceremony and the eighth-grade memory book. They were a part of the prophecy that year because the eighth-grade writers knew them well enough to joke about them. They had all gone on the traditional trip to Springfield, which David, along with the seventh- and eighth-grade teachers, chaperoned. The special ed kids also participated in the annual graduates' picnic, which offered games, contests, a ritual, high-stakes tug-of-war that ended in a soaking for one team, and finally, a community cookout with hot dogs, hamburgers, and very mushy, melted, sloppy somemores. They had mingled at the more formal graduation party held at a restaurant not far from school. In their dress-up clothes, they danced to the music selections of a disk jockey, and they made some requests of their own.

They contributed their goals to the yearbook staff. Miriam's ambition was "to work in a hospital that provides hearing aids to deaf children." David, from the communication-disorders class, was destined for fame. It was prophesied that he "would be discovered by an advertising agent because of his smile, and his picture would be seen on every dentist's wall." Shy and quiet Luke "would create world peace and harmony through his good nature and peaceful ways." Ridiculously, in four short years Chris would grow from a five-foot-tall boy to a seven-foot-tall basketball player for the Chicago Bulls.

And at the formal graduation ceremony in the Kennedy High School auditorium, where every student was in the royal blue of caps and gowns and every mother held a Kleenex along with a camera, Maria, who was deaf, gave a speech. Semara, from the severe-learning-disabilities class, sang a solo. It was a beautiful graduation, and a warm and welcoming reception followed for all.

CHAPTER 23

The process to get a child removed from the regular class is long and referrals are carefully considered, so why are we just putting kids back in with no consideration of progress they've made?

Attorney Jay Kraning

(The child) should not have to earn his way into an integrated school setting by first functioning successfully in a segregated setting," said the judge. "Inclusion is a right, not a privilege for a select few.

New Jersey Federal Court

The battle of inclusion had begun. According to records filed with the U.S. Department of Education, 5500 children with disabilities were placed in regular classes in Chicago in 1991 and 1992. City principals and teachers were beginning to complain that the central office was not providing the staffing or the support they needed to teach these disabled students, particularly those with behavioral disorders and emotional disturbances. In some of the worst situations, severely emotionally disturbed children were being placed in already overcrowded classrooms.

Operation PUSH, Jesse Jackson's neighborhood organization, accused the Chicago school system of "dumping" disabled kids in regular classes. In response, the associate superintendent of special education services, Dr. Thomas Hehir, admitted that some kids had been put in schools without resources, but he explained that he had investigated all complaints and added services when they were needed. Dr. Hehir countered that most schools were complying willingly with system initiatives if they were given the resources. Some schools, however, were resisting inclusion, and they needed monitoring and intervention. "When you have a well-trained principal and a well-functioning school council, they don't need us very much. But some schools don't want to serve certain types of kids, or don't know how to, and someone has to watch those schools and safeguard those children's rights."

Some of Kinzie's former students returned to visit. They showed past teachers their new high-school schedules, which contained three or four study halls per day. These students were in dire need of remedial classes and small group tutoring, not distracting, auditorium-size study halls in which monitors spent forty-five minutes taking attendance because of the number of children. The rumor was circulating that the city's foremost deaf high school center was going to be disbanded. Their Local School Council no longer wanted responsibility for the citywide deaf program. In addition, in keeping with the inclusion policy, deaf children were being encouraged to attend schools near their homes. Their parents were being urged to consider the small programs that were starting up in scattered neighborhoods of the city. In some schools students who had never been mainstreamed for academic classes because they had multiple learning problems and were reading at the primary level were to be *included* in freshman history and algebra classes and have the opportunity to learn cosmetology and auto repair. Gathering a critical mass of students for a viable high school program was no longer a priority. The inclusion movement was touching even deaf students now.

Kinzie teachers and parents questioned the future of deaf programs for Chicago students. Brenton's mother was one

Kinzie parent who was anxiously examining the alternatives for her son's high school placement. Brenton had been a rubella baby. Not only was he profoundly deaf, but also, even after cataract surgery, he had no vision in his left eye except for a sensitivity to light. Along with a congenital heart defect, he suffered from asthma. Initially his problems were just too complex for his sixteen-year-old mother to manage, and she rarely had the wherewithal to obtain the resources available to her.

Now at the age of twelve, Brenton was reading at the first-grade level and receiving learning-disabilities services from David. His speech was labeled unintelligible, his signing skills determined to be low level, and his social-reasoning ability considered below average. He had a history of spitting, hitting, and kicking kids and staff. These days he frequently got into fights on the bus and often made obscene gestures at anyone he encountered. Although he needed glasses and a hearing aid, he rarely had them and was a case for medical neglect. He had been recommended for a behavior disorder classroom, but his mother never followed through. Brenton's attention span seemed to be improving a little with his age. Sometimes he could function productively. His one area of strength was problem solving involving assembly skills. Unbelievably, dance emerged as another of Brenton's talents.

Brenton attended Kinzie's first summer arts camp. He auditioned for and won the solo role as the Scarecrow in the *Wizard of Oz*. To the consternation and relief of the staff, he responded to the challenge, took responsibility for learning his lines, and relished his rare positive recognition. He began to dance, hesitantly at first; but then he happily discovered that his thin and wiry body was suited to the exercises. Gradually, his enthusiasm expanded and transformed itself into commitment. Brenton became a leader in the dance activities.

He, Darren, Adrian, James, and several other students, who were at times Kinzie's "wild boys," formed an athletic, creative, and talented corps that began to choreograph their own dances under the leadership of Rosemary Doolas.

Rosemary was a professional dancer and the director of the Chicago Dance Medium, a small performance company based in the Fine Arts Building. Rosemary, a true artist, moved in a realm of dance far apart from the educational establishment. Consequently, in order to select her students, she didn't consult the various evaluations in their voluminous cumulative folders. She looked instead at *them,* recognizing their exuberance of movement and willingness to work hard.

No one worked harder than Rosemary herself. Tiny, but jam-packed with energy, she wouldn't allow even hip replacement surgery to keep her off the dance floor for very long. Her first residency at Kinzie, *Colors That Bend,* was a modern dance program interpreting the poetry of the painter Wassily Kandinsky, and it was supported by the Illinois Arts Council. During that semester Rosemary touched all of Kinzie's students because every single child participated in this project in one way or another. Each class studied one of the poems from Kandinsky's book. They illustrated it, recited it individually or in groups, and their best students performed it in an assembly. At the same time, the art classes constructed gigantic painted figures that sprang to life from the imagery of the poems, and they splashed and dabbled rainbow compositions in the abstract style of the artist. Kandinsky prints and Kandinsky look-alikes brightened all the halls.

Then came *Always Walk in the Lunchroom Unless Somebody Tells You to Run,* the culminating performance of the residency. Kinzie students, together with the Chicago Dance Medium professionals, created a lively modern dance collection that they offered to the community on a Saturday night in the Kennedy High School auditorium. Ticket sales were fairly brisk and the reviews favorable.

> The children from our school put forth so much energy, you had to love it! We watched the youngsters warm up and strut their stuff. If I were a critic, I'd give the professional dancers an 8 and the Kinzie students a 10!
> Rozanne, eighth grade

Like Jacques D'Amboise in the ghettos of New York City, Rosemary was introducing hearing and deaf children in Chicago to the spontaneity and passion of her art form—dance. Students whose families could never have afforded dance lessons responded to the contagion of her artistic curiosity. Some leapt through Friday Afternoon Activities, tumbled and jumped after school, and even spun downtown in the Chicago Dance Medium studios. Their commitment required a sacrifice on the part of their parents to get them to these practices, but in the end they were allowed to perform in concert with the company in the Fine Arts Building. Following their very successful debut, they attended a gala reception in the CDM studio. Dressed in frilly party dresses or white shirts and ties, these student dancers, along with their parents, nibbled on finger sandwiches and hors d'oeuvres to the accompaniment of a classical string quartet. Through the open windows of the dance studio, they gazed out on the sparkling splashes of colors shooting like fireworks from the illuminated Buckingham Fountain. It was a magical spring night, a panorama far different from the familiar view of their project homes only a few miles away.

PROJECT

People live in
Rooms full
Of family and
Junk, baby clothes, food, toys.
Elevators go up to
Crowded apartments and
Touch more floors.

Cecilia, deaf, fifth grade

The following summer brought Kinzie's first arts-camp production of the *Wizard of Oz*. Reminiscent of the old Judy Garland–Mickey Rooney movies, the kids rewrote the classic story into a play, personalizing its plot to include a tornado tossing Kinzie School into the Oz Amusement Park. The kids, under the direction of Marilyn, Barbara Ridgeway, and Glor, concocted outlandish costumes and far-out sets, and they energetically performed in the play and in dance production numbers.

The following fall Brenton and his classmates went on to choreograph their own basketball dance, which they performed at Chicago's new Harold Washington Library. Their concert with the Chicago Dance Medium was broadcast as one segment of a dance series on cable television. Rosemary continued her classes, and the Kinzie Dance Project evolved, a student performing company funded by the Chicago Neighborhood Arts Program. It was Rosemary's dream, which she made come true. With a backbone of steel herself, she was forcing her student dancers to self-discipline and control, to goal setting. Some of the children, including Brenton, rose to the challenge, then intermittently regressed. But Rosemary would not give up on them. A unique relationship developed between dance teacher and students. Their hard work and resulting accomplishments in dance ultimately raised the level of these children's self-esteem enough to spill over into the classroom where their learning behaviors exhibited more responsibility.

The second summer, arts camp enrollment quadrupled! Rosemary, Barbara Ridgeway, Marilyn Steiner, and I offered drama, dance, art, and writing to each of four age groups, for four weeks, and for approximately four hours each day. The schedule was intense; the theme was "how does it feel to be a building." In writing, I had the children building verses.

Forces Squeeze

Fist fight
Hug tight
Toothpaste ooze
Pillow snooze
Muscle lump
Pencil finger bump
Sponge puffy
Teddy Bear fluffy
Freeze pop slurp
Juice box burp
Bat smash
Hand bash
Water balloon pop
Brother's neck—STOP!
Summer Camp Super Poets: David, Meaghan, Kate, Allison,
John, Nicole, Joel

In art Marilyn took the kids from sand castles to huge jerry-built houses for the three pigs, with plenty of paper, straw, stick, clay, and you-name-it buildings in-between. In drama Barbara dynamically directed "The Three Pigs" and "The Real Story of the Three Pigs."

Rosemary had Brenton and his colleagues so motivated that summer that they chose choreography over basketball and outside recess. And in the fall the Kinzie Dance Project was invited to perform at Universal Studios, Florida, in a national New Year's Gala dance production. The kids eagerly anticipated a side trip to Disney World for one day, but we just weren't able to raise the money for airfare.

Summer of 1992 included not only arts camp for the kids but also our first series of planning meetings for teachers to integrate the curriculum. With a small grant from the Foundation for Educational Reform we began at the primary level. Teachers rearranged units to correlate social studies and reading or science and math when appropriate. A new feeling of camaraderie evolved as first-grade teachers shared ideas for language units, second-grade teachers planned a year of hands-on science activities, and third-grade teachers organized social studies around literature. Regular and special ed teachers collaborated more closely than they ever had before. *At last* there was real time for teachers to plan *together*.

In the fall preparation periods were arranged so that grade-level meetings would occur each month, and teachers could exchange techniques and materials that worked. These cooperative-planning meetings were initiated at four levels, and they focused on the needs specific to each group. Primary teachers spent most of their time sharing ideas and solving problems that arose from the new literature-based reading series. Preschool teachers developed strategies for getting more parent involvement. Intermediate teachers focused on classroom-management techniques; and at the upper grade levels, they discussed departmental concerns and the various schoolwide projects including the science fair, the academic bowl, the new student council, and the drug awareness program.

Kinzie came to the attention of the Northern Illinois University Department of Education. Their practice students had been reporting how warmly they were accepted into the Kinzie community, how easily they acquired assistance and direction from teachers willing to share their expertise and experience. The university reached out to form a partnership. If we would commit to accepting a specified number of practice teachers, they would offer us teacher training and university expertise in projects like our current move to integrate the curriculum; in sum, it was a symbiotic contract we couldn't refuse.

At the same time the *Southtown Economist* newspaper agreed to provide mentors to Kinzie students. A reporter, photographer, editor, and sales director provided our kids with the know-how to become a newspaper staff. Seventh- and eighth-grade boys and girls, including Kenith, Jenni, and Sergio, planned and produced a school newspaper that was delivered by Kinzie paperboys to every home in our school attendance area. It was a tremendous opportunity to touch the community, to involve more residents in our Local School Council activities.

Excitedly, the kids sold and designed ads for neighborhood stores. Looking at the newspaper as a business that had to support itself was a perspective we had never considered. The students managed to raise $280, in tough economic times, from a local restaurant, a bike shop, a resale clothing store, a bookseller, and from private donors. Enthusiastically, the students wrote news stories about our basketball team, which started the season with a win! and our volleyball team, which still hadn't lost a game in a series of five. An editorial on the overcrowding problems in the lunchroom brought about a schedule change. There were also features on new teachers and a Kinzie student hero. Karla, a third grader, had saved a preschooler who slipped through a gap in the playground apparatus from choking. Kids also reviewed their favorite TV programs and reported on the year's new Friday Afternoon Activities.

Jenni wrote about being deaf:

I remember the day I asked my mom, "Why did I have to be deaf?"

She said my deafness could have been family-heredity. And she told me that I should be happy that I have a hearing aid to help me hear better. She also said, "It's better to be deaf than blind because a hearing aid helps you to hear, and there isn't any way to make blind people see." Then I accepted my deafness.

I get a lot of benefits using my hearing aid. I get to hear all the sounds that I never heard before. The greatest thing is listening to music. That relaxes me. To shut the noises out of my head, I can always take my hearing aid off.

Sometimes it's difficult to make friends with hearing kids. My mom encouraged me to try and I did. Now I'm communicating well with the hearing kids, even sometimes in our class they will sign or fingerspell to me or to their other friends. It is cool and great.

At home I'm the third deaf generation in my mom's family. My grandparents, uncle, mom, dad, and my brother are also deaf. To communicate we use sign language.

To call someone we use a TDD, a special machine to communicate, like a telephone and typewriter combined. We have flashing lights to tell us that the phone or doorbell is ringing. We also have closed-caption words on our TV so we can understand what the characters are saying.

I am happy to be what I am. I am not ashamed of myself. I want the whole world to know that deaf people can do anything except hear.

Jenni, seventh grade

There was a flat, cerulean-painted sea with just a few white, wavy lines scattered across its wide expanse. The ocean covered three-fourths of the paper. In the upper left hand corner, a big, round, yellow ball of a sun pointed all of its rays to a spot just about center. There, skimming along the upper edge of the sea, was a bulging yellow submarine. Musical notes were flying out of its outline. Two tiny, green islands were planted at opposite ends of the picture, one to the east and one to the west.

Mr. Franklin initiated regular committee meetings to determine the future role of American Sign Language in Kinzie's educational program. Everyone was familiar with *Unlocking the Curriculum,* by Johnson, Liddell, and Erting (Washington, D.C.: Gallaudet Research Institute, 1989); and all of us had experienced the practical problems anticipated with the use of this model. The authors advocated a curriculum in which all children first became competent in American Sign Language and then later learned English through second-language instruction. We knew that less than 10 percent of our students had deaf parents. Only a few children had any early exposure to American Sign Language, and the Kinzie faculty was not fluent in ASL either. Terry was our only deaf teacher. Also, counter to the bilingual/bicultural approach, speech, speechreading, and auditory training had always been integral parts of our educational program. But despite these real school conflicts, we were examining the ASL option. Improving our deaf students' language skills had always been our primary goal and literacy our strongest wish. Most of us had already made one major transformation, from the oral approach to the utilization of total communication, signed English. We felt that it had been a positive change for the children, and we were willing to make some changes again if it was in their best interests.

Kayla Ruskin, a preschool teacher, Ms. Brownell, and Donna and Veda, who were hearing parents of deaf children and interpreters, visited a bilingual/bicultural program in Indiana. They reported their mixed impressions to the ASL committee. Discontinuing amplification and relegating speech instruction, spoken English, to a brief period once a week were practices directly opposed to our current philosophy.

Deaf staff members, Terry, Patti, and Barbara Peters, offered the insights of their own family and educational experiences, which, even within this small group, varied widely. School personnel read divergent articles on ASL and language instruction gleaned from the full spectrum of deaf education resources, from the A. G. Bell Association, with its newsletters highlighting oral successes and participation in mainstream American culture, to *TBC News* with its call for "bi-bi" (bilingual/bicultural) separatism and total submersion in deaf culture, including ASL.

We arrived at the same conclusions and the same questions as Dr. Larry Newman in addressing the 1990 Conference, "Bilingual Considerations in the Education of Deaf Students: ASL and English":

> We can't pigeonhole a deaf person into one square. We have to think of the different settings in which people were raised. But we have to look at reality and ask such questions as: How do we help deaf children learn skills in English? How can we overcome the barriers to learning

English? If children learn ASL and then switch over, will that learning be transferred to written English?

We are still meeting on ASL; we haven't agreed yet on a change of methodology. We are considering ways to modify or add to the programs we have built over the past ten years, our mainstream programs in which we take pride. We are contemplating a pilot preschool program utilizing ASL and adhering to the constraints of a genuine research project. For the present we are all in training. Terry is continuing American Sign Language classes for teachers, but no hearing teacher is proficient in ASL yet. Kayla is close, and there are other teachers in interpreter training programs. Our interpreters are increasing their ASL skills. No other deaf teachers have arrived at Kinzie School. A more formal Deaf Culture program for teachers and students is beginning. We are inspired by the remarks of Dr. I. King Jordan, president of Gallaudet University.

Bilingual and bicultural. To me this means two things at once. These terms indicate an equality. Both languages and both cultures demanding equal recognition and equal respect. We must foster that attitude—we must demand that practice and that environment of respect for both American Sign Language and English. We must also have equal respect for both mainstream American culture and the rich legacy of deaf culture.

We look at hearing children signing to their deaf classmates and recognize that there is already acceptance of deaf culture and sign language at Kinzie.

For the second year, Kinzie School was named a model school for *inclusion* by the Chicago Board of Education. Again, although the focus of inclusion is home school placement, the bureau of special education considered the critical-mass factor and the unique needs of deaf children in determining the character of appropriate programs for deaf students. Its approach was more tempered than that of numerous school boards in the suburbs of Chicago. Many special education programs have already disbanded, and hospital beds have been moved into regular classrooms. The instruction of children with special needs, in numerous cases, has fallen upon the shoulders of a teacher aide or in some situations where no aide is available, on a regular student. Often too, children with disabilities are spending as much time in the halls as they are in class because they are too disruptive in the regular classroom, and their special education classes have been closed.

I observed a student who needed intense language remediation at the primary level coloring ditto pictures of Indians in a fifth-grade classroom because he was included there, but he was incapable of participating in the intermediate activities of their social studies unit. Across the hall in another fifth-grade class, a trained teacher of deaf students was interpreting all day for a ten-year-old child who was deaf. District personnel had only identified his hearing loss a few months earlier. Because of his age he was placed in a fifth-grade room where the rapid flow of signed English meant absolutely nothing to him. Although his teacher had been directed to include this child in the intermediate curriculum in just this manner, in inconspicuous ways during the day she tried to teach him basic vocabulary. The principal of this school could not say enough about the good feelings generated by inclusion, children happily pushing wheelchairs, enthusiastically learning to sign "Hello. How are you?"

And that is the thrust of inclusion—feelings, not academics. Inclusion is an issue of the heart, not the brain. It is a dream, an attitude, an issue of morality. Attending a seminar on inclusion is akin to a revival. The child with special needs is freed of them. He is not disabled but "differently-abled." Mainstreaming and integration are unacceptable because their goal is to make all children fit into the mainstream culture. Special education should be abolished because special education teachers do nothing different from regular teachers. We need only one system of education, and we need not focus on achievement. If we build our students' characters, their scores will rise. Inclusion means love, compassion, joy, and community, the acceptance of all children's differences.

Inclusion, in the reality of our current educational system, means fear, confusion, neglect, and fragmentation. The supporting framework is lacking. In the fall of 1992 Kinzie presented "Mainstreaming and Meaningful Inclusion" at the state conference of the Illinois Council for Exceptional Children. Ms. Brownell, Glor, Mary Kay, and I once again discussed our experiences in developing Kinzie's various mainstream programs. Mr. Franklin delivered an impassioned plea to administrators to consider carefully the program decisions they were making and to use educational common sense. He urged that academics not be abandoned in placement selections, and that the interests of both regular and special students be weighed when programs are initiated. Our group reminded those present that the law mandated an education "appropriate" for the child with disabilities. Appropriate meant the availability of a full spectrum of classroom placements, from fully included to self-contained.

Kinzie staff members pointed out that the programs initiated at our school illustrate how children with special needs can be mainstreamed unconditionally into the school environment without being integrated for all of their academic subjects. In a child-focused program they can still receive all of the special services they need to make them as independent as possible. They can also emulate deaf role models among the staff members and become assimilated into deaf culture.

Kinzie School is that yellow submarine. It has weathered several stormy seas and is now skimming along a calm surface, confident that it is meeting the individual needs of its passengers, who are happily signing and singing along their trip. Reform has given Kinzie the freedom to determine its own course. Across the cerulean blue expanse one can see in opposite directions two little islands. To the east is the encapsulating ring of Bi-Bi, to the west the sandy diffusion of Inclusion. Both erupted suddenly to the surface of the sea from a volatile volcano of civil rights. Reform has given Kinzie the freedom to determine its own course.

CHAPTER 25

Hi! My name is Amy. I'm a handicapped child.
Amy, primary communication disorders class

Amy was not shy. Once she was enrolled in Kinzie's primary communication disorders class, she introduced herself to everyone she encountered on the playground, in the halls, and the lunchroom. She repeated, practically shouting, "Hi! My name is Amy. I'm a handicapped child." After she was here for a few months, I met Amy in the office. She marched right up to the counter, and in a very loud voice sang out, "Hi! My name is Amy. I'm a Brownie."

Amy is just one example of how a school can be programmed for success.

Mr. Franklin received the Whitman Award for Excellence in Educational Administration in 1990. His nomination letter was signed by the entire staff.

Kinzie's Local School Council was recognized by the Ameritech Bell Foundation in its first year search for schools where reform had improved the educational program. A monetary grant of $10,000 was included to assist in the implementation of LSC programs. Because of the Ameritech Award, Channel 11, WTTW, featured Kinzie's band and especially its deaf members in a 1990 series of shorts entitled *Schools That Work*.

In 1992 Northern Illinois University selected Kinzie as a model training-site for its student teachers and interns in deaf education.

Markeeta was chosen the most outstanding child with a disability in the state of Illinois. The 1989 award was named for her, and each year since the "Markeeta" has been given to a different exceptional child.

Barbara Ridgeway was named the Rookie Teacher of the Year for 1990 by the Illinois Council for Exceptional Children. She and Kayla Ruskin were recognized for participation in a special Chicago Summer Arts Program, 1993.

Ms. Krachic, the LSC chair, was selected the outstanding parent volunteer in our District. Her twenty-five years of dedication to the programs at Kinzie School were acknowledged in 1992.

Ms. Strager won a trip to Washington, D.C., with other Power Hour Parents in 1991. She was recognized for her work with scouts during Friday Afternoon Activities. Not only did the Brownie troop expand, but Ms. Strager started Junior Girl Scouts and Daisies. She motivated many mothers to join in and help on Friday afternoons.

Joey's speech continues to improve, and his progress in mainstream classes merits him honor-roll status. This year he is the captain of his hockey team as well as the lead in the lip-sync opera. He had a small part in a professional theater production.

Jennifer is in pompons, the newspaper staff, and band. Like every seventh grader, she continues to be extremely sensitive about relationships with her classmates, but she is usually encircled by boys and girls, hearing and deaf. Her new best friend is Rose.

Sergio is quietly excelling in seventh-grade math and music. He is on the high honor roll in all of his subjects and was nominated for an I Can award in 1992.

Edward had surgery in 1993. We're anxiously waiting for his return and hoping that he will be able to travel around the school more easily now.

Brenton continues to excel in dance. His academic achievement is still below grade level, but his attitude, motivation, and study skills have improved slightly. His mother is considering the state residential school for Brenton's high school years.

Members of the Illinois Teachers of the Hearing Impaired have requested an informational meeting with board personnel regarding high school programs for deaf children, and they are considering changing their name.

Friday Afternoon Activities received a commendation from the Chicago Citizens Schools Committee in 1993.

The primary communication arts class created one of the top six books submitted nationwide to Children's Book Fairs in 1992.

The very first communication arts class continues to check in. Trina won art and drama awards in high school. She volunteered at summer arts camp, and the kids loved her. Tara flew off to Europe for a year. She attended an arts-oriented high school, worked at the nearby Candlelight Theater while she was in school, and plans a dramatic career of some sort, perhaps in costuming. Olivia came back to Kinzie to perform for our students; she was confident enough to do several solo dances. She was one of the leaders in the dance program at Whitney Young High School.

The Kinzie Dance Project missed its chance to perform at Universal Studios in Orlando, Florida. We just weren't able to raise the ten thousand dollars we needed for expenses.

Mary Kay Sandusky, Marilyn Steiner, and Diana Sandler won 1993 grants from the Chicago Foundation for Education. Mary Kay's students received various poetry awards.

Laura Miller continues to monitor the compliance of the board in the provision of speech services to deaf children. Before she filed her complaint, only 4 percent of Chicago's deaf students received speech therapy. Today 60 percent of those students are getting speech services from speech-and-language pathologists.

Dr. Hehir resigned and returned to his home state. He has left public education for consulting.

I received the Golden Apple Award for Excellence in Teaching, and with it came a sabbatical in 1991 to write this book. *All of Us Together* is my effort to recognize all of the members of the Kinzie community who have helped create a nurturing school environment, one that is a setting for meaningful inclusion.

CHAPTER 26

We would sit around and wait for the mail to come in and just talk. And the deaf would be there, everyone would be there. And they were part of the crowd, and they were accepted. They were fishermen and farmers and everything else. And they wanted to find out the news just as much as the rest of us. And often, people would tell stories and make signs at the same time so everyone could follow him together. Of course, sometimes, if there were more deaf than hearing there, everyone would speak sign language—just to be polite, you know.

Martha's Vineyard

Martha's Vineyard, an island five miles off the southeastern coast of Massachusetts, was first settled by Europeans around 1640. Mostly Englishmen and Wampanoag Indians created a rapidly growing community. There were very few "off-island" marriages, and hereditary deafness occurred at a rate many times higher than that of the national population. In the nineteenth century one out of every 2,730 Americans was born deaf. On Martha's Vineyard the rate was one out of every 155. In the little village of Chillmark, with a population of 500, one in every 25 individuals was deaf. In one section of that village, 1 of every 4 people was deaf. Everyone knew and used sign language. It was the natural thing to do.